HAVE I
EVER TOLD YOU?

Sylvia Lindsay

HAVE I
EVER TOLD YOU?

Thoughts AND *Reminiscences*
OF A BELOVED MOTHER

Sylvia Lindsay

AMBASSADOR INTERNATIONAL
GREENVILLE, SOUTH CAROLINA & BELFAST, NORTHERN IRELAND

www.ambassador-international.com

Have I Ever Told You?
Thoughts and Reminiscences of a Beloved Mother

ISBN: 978-1-62020-723-9
eISBN: 978-1-62020-757-4

Cover Design and Page Layout by Hannah Nichols
eBook Conversion by Anna Riebe Raats

Unless otherwise indicated, Bible quotations are taken from the King James Version, copyright © Cambridge University Press and Oxford University Press 1961, 1970. All rights reserved.

AMBASSADOR INTERNATIONAL
Emerald House
411 University Ridge, Suite B14
Greenville, SC 29601, USA
www.ambassador-international.com

AMBASSADOR BOOKS
The Mount
2 Woodstock Link
Belfast, BT6 8DD, Northern Ireland, UK
www.ambassadormedia.co.uk

The colophon is a trademark of Ambassador, a Christian publishing company.

Contents

Photo Album

Part Two

Chapter 1

ANCESTRY

IT PRESENTS A MOST DIFFICULT TASK to write of a dear Mother who has been blessed with a long stay on this earth, whose life has touched so many people in all walks of life, a life of contrasts, a sparkling stream could soon be a storm-tossed sea.

Born in a town enjoying the hustle and bustle of urban life, only seeing as far as the house opposite, or living in the country thrilling with every breath of pure fresh air with a glorious vista for miles around.

Delivering milk in streets where poverty was rife, seeing the troubled wife whose husband had drunk the last penny, with crying hungry children clinging to her skirt or what was left of it, or tending the tennis and croquet lawns of the landed gentry with their exquisite manners and prancing horses and carriages.

Living and working amongst those who had no faith or attending places of worship with those who loved the Lord with all their heart.

Going down on her knees to be on the same level as a little child to persuade him to say a Sunday School anniversary piece or standing up to the farmers who persistently allowed their cattle to graze her pastures and tried to steal her sheep.

Keeping a lone vigil shedding silent tears pleading with her Lord and nursing her own beloved child fighting for his last breath or taking on manual farm labour to earn enough to enable her own children to one day farm their own land.

Making and mending clothes for those without means to buy essential garments or dining at the table of titled gentry.

Perhaps this precious life of such a beloved one can be summed up in her favourite Psalm, **"Because thou hast made the LORD, *which is* my refuge, *even* the most high, thy habitation; there shall no evil befall thee, neither shall any plague come nigh thy dwelling. For he shall give his angels charge over thee, to keep thee in all thy ways." Psalm 91:9-11.**

Vera Emmeline Charter was born on September 11, 1910. She was one of the youngest of five children born to Arthur Thomas Charter, who was born August 10, 1875, and Mary Elizabeth Ann Charter, born April 2, 1873. Rosalind was nearly five years younger.

Their son, Everard Leavesley, was born March 10, 1901; followed two years later by twins, William and John; alas John, did not survive; sister, Lilian Mary, first saw the light of day on March 2, 1906 with Vera Emmeline appearing nearly five years later; then along came Rosalind Rachel on the December 6, 1914.

Vera was the only one to enter into matrimony.

Arthur Charter was born at 30 Eastgate, Driffield in North Yorkshire. He served his apprenticeship with Sheperdson's in Driffield then with Lawrence's Cabinet Makers in Nottingham. It was reported that a gentleman brought into the factory a Chippendale Chair for repair; Arthur repaired the chair which was placed amongst new ones; when the owner came to collect it he did not know which was his.

The apprentices had to make their own tool chests which were about the size of a blanket box or large ottoman with drawers in various sizes and removable compartments. Arthur took a great deal of time and his box was ornate, something that brought much pleasure to Vera as a child. On hearing one day that the factory was on fire Arthur and his friend raced to the blazing building and rescued their toolboxes.

Arthur was a Methodist local preacher and, while in Nottingham, was invited regularly to the home of the Thornhill family, also Methodists. Mr.

John Thornhill was a singer of renown as well as a preacher. One day Mary Elizabeth Ann Thornhill, John's eldest daughter, who had been working away from home as a children's maid for some time, went to the chapel were her father was to preach; she was sitting quietly before the service when she heard the voices of some lads at the back who had not recognised her.

A voice piped up, "Dis tha knaw Thornhill wat soort of a preacher is he?"

"Oh he's nowt of a preacher. It's his singing that taks."

Such a love for the Methodists had Lily that nearly every Lord's Day you would find her pouring over her Methodist Hymn book.

Lily spoke of her early years of carol singing, walking arm in arm, crunching through the snow. Her eyes would light up, no one knowing exactly what memories were flooding through her mind.

Lily's only claim to fame was that her cousin, Harry Churchill Beet, was awarded a Victoria Cross. On February 18, 1892, he joined the Sherwood Foresters in Derby, at eighteen years of age. By 1896, he was a lance corporal. He studied hard to gain his stripes. From 1897 to 1899, he served in India, receiving the India General Service Medal with clasps: PUNJAB FRONTIER 1897-98 and TIRAH 1897-98. The outbreak of the Boer War resulted in Corporal Beet being sent to South Africa where he distinguished himself by his gallant conduct.

On April 22, 1900 at Wakkerstroom in the Orange Free State, Number Two Mounted Infantry Company, First Battalion of the Derbyshire Regiment, two squadrons of the Imperial Yeomanry found themselves below Boers who were on a ridge above them; they were under accurate and continuous fire. Eventually, they retired to a nearby farm. Basil Burnett, a corporal in the Yeomanry, was so badly wounded he could not join the retreat. He was shot in the hip and lay unable to move. Harry Beet dragged him to cover and bound up his wounds as best he could; he stayed with him until it was dark. Although the accurate fire continued, his skill and courage kept the Boers from advancing to the Farm. Under the cover of darkness, a doctor came and dealt with the wounded man's injuries and all escaped. Basil Burnett wrote to thank Harry Beet in February 1901.

For his gallantry Lily's cousin was awarded the Victoria Cross. He emigrated in 1914 and lived on a ranch in Saskatchewan. During World War One he enlisted in Saskatchewan and was made a Battery Sergeant Major.

When World War Two came, at the age of sixty-seven, he joined the 110th Infantry Reserve Company. He was discharged in 1942; he was not happy, as the war was still on in Japan.

Harry Beet joined the Royal Canadian Mounted Police as a guard at a Japanese Internment Camp. He died in 1946.

Her grandmother on her paternal side was named Bean and on her maternal side, Beet, so she said she was a little cabbage.

John Thornhill, Lily's Father, lived at 8 Meadow Cottages Netherfield; he worked with the Railways and also, part of his life, as a Wagoner.

On a visit to the Thornhills, Arthur gave up his chair when Mary Elizabeth Ann, known as Lily to her family, entered. She had a beautiful countenance. When she later moved to Driffield it was widely argued over which was the most beautiful woman in Driffield at that time: Lily or a wife of one of the doctors. As she took the chair, she noticed Arthur had a twinkle in his eye.

She thought to herself, "It's no use looking here. Arthur. I'm not interested." Eventually she married him on June 8, 1900.

Arthur wrote to say he was marrying Lily. The reply from his father was, "Come home, lad, and take over my dairy business. It's too much for me." Not realising it then that it was the end of his cabinet making, it was also a final curtain of the "Life of a Lady" for his new bride. It was a heart ache for Lily to leave her family; although, she worked away from home for some years. In those days of horse drawn vehicles and few trains Nottingham and Yorkshire were a world apart.

Lily was a gentle soul; one who could look at a crochet garment in a shop window and go home and copy it exactly—until misfortune struck. Arriving home from work one weekend she went to her drawer that contained years of exquisite work to find it empty.

"Mam, have you moved my crochet work?"

"Yes. I gave it to your sister as a wedding present."

The pain was too much to bear and Lily was never known to do any crochet work again.

After a honeymoon spent in Wales, the wedded couple made their way north, where they made their home in Victoria Road before moving to Westgate then to No 1 Middle Street North to a house known as "Nut shell" in later years. It caused great amusement when a gentleman called at the house and asked if the Colonel (kernel) was in.

Lily, being of such a gentle and sweet disposition, took hardly to the rigours of cows, muddy boots, and the rough Yorkshire country life; in addition, she was expected to trudge round the town taking milk to the doors which was so much against her fragile nature, but the one thing that was to remain with her throughout the rest of her life was her undying devotion to her husband. Although he tried her to the limit, she thought the world of him and him alone.

Lily's sisters, Amy, Annie, and Meg, all married and stayed in the Nottinghamshire area; her sister Hannah married and moved to Portsmouth. It was seldom, if ever, these two would ever meet again. Although every Christmas and birthday, Lily received a beautiful garment, a lacy bed jacket, or some such delicate article. (making up for the loss of her crochet?)

Her brothers, Arthur and Bert, with their wives and families visited Driffield often, which brought great joy to Lily. One heart break she never got over was the death of her brother, John Willie, aged fourteen. He had been playing football on the Lord's Day and injured his leg but dare not tell his devout mother and father. He was taken to the doctor, no one knowing what the swelling was. The doctor told his mother to massage it, which she faithfully did—only to tell the doctor one day that she was going to massage it no more as she was making it worse; alas it was too late. He died when a blood clot reached his heart.

Arthur was one of a family of nine. His brother, Walter, and his wife, Annie, were poulterers and lived in Providence Place, Driffield. John and wife, Doris, had no family but had a grocers shop in Victoria Road. Sister, Annie, and her husband, Alf Robson, farmed at Wansford. Polly and Lily Charter never married and were dressmakers working from their home at 30 Eastgate Driffield. Emily married John Wilson, who had a paper hanging business, first in Exchange Street moving later to Middle Street. Arthur was a twin and his sister, Ada, was renowned for her beautiful clothes and gold jewelry. She married Charlie Wren and had a painters and decorators business at Withernsea. Sally married Jack Reynolds and had no family; they were cabinet makers living in Scarborough Road.

For Lily it was like moving to a hornets' nest as all Arthur's family lived close by. With Arthur being one of the youngest, many of his nephews and nieces were grown up when Lily met them.

On returning to Driffield with his sweet wife, Arthur's dairy business flourished. Arthur had a word for everyone; he had no pride in his appearance whatsoever. On returning from the fields once in a torn old jacket, he met a Salvation Army officer visiting the town. Thinking he was a tramp, the officer gave him a penny, saying, "Here, my friend. This will help you on your way."

He showed friends that penny for many years.

The only exception in his code of dress was the Lord's Day when he was preaching. He loved the starched white fronts so favoured in those days. Lily had to iron these whilst still damp with the flat irons heated on the fire. It was no easy task to keep them spotless. Poor Lily would be in fear and trembling when Arthur went to get changed. All of a sudden, the stairs door would open and even the tiniest blemish would result in the front being hurled across the room with the words "How do you expect a man to wear this?"

This became too much and one day after the outburst she calmly replied, "Well, Arthur, you have no choice. It is the only one you have."

When they were planning the wedding, the subject of the dress came up and Arthur persuaded Lily to let Polly, his sister, make her dress. Although not entirely happy with this, Lily gave him the money for the dress. All was well until one day sometime after the wedding, there was a disagreement between Lily and Polly.

Polly in an outburst said, "Oh, you had nothing when you married Arthur. He even had to pay for your wedding dress."

In total horror Lily cried, "No, he did not! I gave him the money." This unfortunately described her husband very well.

Lily's father did come to Driffield on numerous occasions, and while Lily was delighted to see him, it annoyed her that as soon as they had their tea, he would get up and say, "I'll just go down and see how Lily and Polly are getting on." He would return in time for supper and to go to bed. This was a regular occurrence.

Some years this went on then his wife, Lily's mother, passed away. He came to Driffield and as usual after tea, "I'll just away and see how Lily and Polly are getting on. "It was not long before he was back, each night the same thing happened, before he left, he said, "I won't be going to see Lily and Polly again. Something has happened they are not the same."

"No" Lily said, "Mother has died. You are a free man and they do not want a husband." Lily was both amused and delighted she had got her father back.

It was a very rare occasion that the timid wife was known to stand up to him. Arthur's father would open the door of their home and throw in an armful of fowl for his poulterer's business with the usual growl of, "Dress these for us, lad."

Slam went the door. This was done on a regular basis with no remuneration. Arthur and Lily now had two young sons and a thriving dairy business.

Lily still helping to deliver milk to the doors, quick as a flash Lily opened the door and threw the fowl back out crying, "Dress your own chickens."

Arthur was in a rage and fell to the floor in a supposed fainting fit. Realising this was a ruse, which could become more frequent, Lily said, "Arthur, never you do that again."

Quietly, she put on her coat, and that of the boys', and set out for Nottingham. Needless to say, she never arrived, and neither was there any more poultry or fainting fits.

By this time, another baby was on the way and Arthur declared to his brother-in-law, Alf Robson—who married Arthur's sister, Annie, in 1884—that he was thinking of buying a pony to deliver milk.

"Thou disn't want a pony. A donkey's good enough for thou."

When Lily heard this she exclaimed, "What a good idea. All the children will want a donkey at the door." This is when beloved Fanny joined the family. Mr. Linsley, a man gifted in working with wood, made a cart that the milk churn would fit in and painted it in bright colours. Arthur fitted bells to the donkey harness and had some soft shoes made; and yes, the children did want the donkey and her livery at their doors. This proved so successful that Arthur purchased another donkey and had a brown one and white one pulling a larger cart, again made by Mr. Linsley. When the Driffield Show came round, Arthur was persuaded to take the donkeys and milk cart round the Show Field in the parade. This was filmed and Arthur was told it was shown at the local cinema. When the donkeys came on the screen, it was reported that the audience rose to their feet and cheered.

Lily, being well read, was willing ears for her nephew, Edwin Robson, when training for a Methodist local preacher. He would take his carefully prepared sermons round for her to hear. Her temperament was such that no criticism only gentle correction if needed would be uttered.

The family was steadily growing. Everard, William, Lilian, and now Vera were making their presence felt.

Chapter 2

VERA AS A CHILD

VERA'S CHILDHOOD WAS NOT WITHOUT MISHAP; one of her earliest memories is of "Madja", her beloved rocking horse from which she was eventually to fall and receive a scar for the rest of her life.

Vera had her schooling days in Driffield. Her brother, Everard, on the first morning took her on the renowned Fanny. Something he ~~were later~~ was later to regret, as afterwards, she wouldn't go to school unless brother was there to take her on the donkey.

The farmstead was in the town. So, obviously the fields were on the outskirts. At four years of age, Vera wandered off and followed her father as he took the cows back to the field after milking. This was very unusual since she was never close to him; although she was very fond of her mother. Unnoticed by family and friends, she toddled after her father and the cows, not knowing her father went home by another way across the fields. When Vera arrived, she was confronted with a locked gate. Mrs. Minns, who lived opposite the field, saw Vera's distressed state, went across, and tried to take her in; but Vera clung to the gate and would not let go. By this time the wee one had been missed at home and Everard (now fourteen), who was very fond of his little sister, set off on his cycle to look for her. As soon as she saw him coming, the troubled soul cried, "Ebedee Ebedee!"

The first words Vera was heard to utter in her cot were what sounded like "Twiggy Voo", a name Everard called her until his death at the age of ninety-three.

When Vera was five years old, she was with her mother and baby sister, Rosalind, (or Rosie as she was better known in the home). Their mother had taken a bowl of boiling curd from the oven and stood it on the floor to cool; picked up the baby to nurse her and asked Vera to bring her slippers. Vera bent to get them from under the sofa. When she stood, she overbalanced and sat in the bowl of curd. Her mother realised what had happened, put the baby down, and tried to take Vera's clothes off, but they had stuck to her burnt peeling skin. Mother called for her husband to fetch the doctor, who arrived. He took one look at Vera said, "She will not live."

Vera said, "I will cos I've prayed."

"And the prayer of faith shall save the sick, and the Lord shall raise him up" James 5:15

Vera did survive only to find thirty years later when her first baby was born the full extent of the internal damage; but once again she survived.

A neighbour's son who regarded Vera with great affection was leaving for duty overseas with the army in the first World War. Benny Abrahams crossed the road to go to see Vera before he left. With tears in his eyes, he said to her mother, "Mrs. Charter, I won't see Vera again."

"Oh, please, don't say that we think she is improving."

"No. I mean I will not be coming home again."

Dear, dear Benny didn't. He was killed in action.

An even stronger bond was found between Mrs. Abrahams and Vera. The little child would go and pick her lovely bouquets of wildflowers, which the dear lady so loved. Mrs. Abraham's would give Vera tasty morsels of her baking.

Every year, on a particularly fine day, her father would suggest a trip to Bridlington. Food would hastily be prepared and packed with the Primus Stove, kettle, tea pot, and containers of water and off they would go. After a particularly enjoyable day on the beach, on the road home in the horse-drawn open-topped phaeton, the family were caught in a heavy thunderstorm. Her father unyoked the horse, tethered her to a gate post, and told the family to get out and go underneath the phaeton for shelter. It was no mean task since it was not very high. After the rains ceased, her father yoked up the horse and off they went on their way, only to find about a hundred yards further on the road that it was perfectly dry. No rain had fallen there. With the seats saturated, they could not sit down. So they were quite a spectacle standing in the carriage: so much so that on the outskirts of Driffield, Lily said, "Arthur stop and put me out. I'll walk home." And she did.

Vera enjoyed her schooldays and was an exceptionally bright pupil who excelled in all lessons. Her learning started at a school in Driffield on the corner of Wansford Road and Nafferton Road. Later she attended the National School on Cross Hill which was established in 1816. She started in standard one, then standard two, missing standard three and going straight to standard four. Standard five missed, standard six straight to standard seven; no mean feat for a dairyman's daughter.

While at school one day, the headmistress came into the class, spoke to the teacher, and proceeded to close the windows and lock the door. The headmistress told the teacher to let no one in or out. The teacher's face went white; however, one of the teachers was able to find a key and was able to help a pupil get outside to go for help. The pupils were eventually evacuated from the building only to learn later that their headmistress had been admitted to the asylum.

When Vera was about twelve years old, the school was awaiting a new headmistress. One day a very small lady walked into the classroom and stood looking around. Vera went to her and asked if she was the new headmistress and then showed her around the school. This was the beginning of a great rapport between these two.

In one arithmetic lesson, Vera could not get a sum right—no matter how hard she tried. The answers were in back of the book and arithmetic being her strongest subject that eventually she went out to Miss Tunnicliffe. She asked her if she would do it. Asking a teacher was one thing, but asking the

Headmistress? Rather indignant at first, she eventually agreed only to find her answer was the same as Vera's and the answer in the book was wrong.

A new teacher arrived: a Miss Kilpatrick, who was a leader apparently in the field of evolution. She told the class that they had evolved from a bit of jelly at the bottom of a pond. Vera put her hand up and said, "My Bible says: **'So God created man in his *own* image, in the image of God created he him; male and female created he them. (Genesis 1:27)'"**

Some very unpleasant words ensued, ending in Vera going to the headmistress, who belonged to the Church of England. It was a Church of England School, and Miss Kilpatrick and her frogspawn did not last long in that atmosphere.

Some years after leaving school, Vera saw Miss Tunnicliffe walking in the town. She ran across the road and after the usual "How are you?", she said, "Oh Vera, I was so looking forward when I heard your sister Rosie was coming into my class, but, oh dear, she is not you."

Treats during and after the 1914-1918 War were few and far between and having strict parents did not make life any easier. At school some children rushed in.

"Vera, come quick! Someone wants you."

Standing at the school gate was Vera's cousin, Frank Charter, in full Military Uniform Red, Black, and Gold. For a schoolgirl, it was too good to be true. She felt so proud of her brave, noble cousin. More than that, he took her to the fair and paid for her to go on some of the rides—something frowned on and forbidden at home; but her father dared not say anything when it was his brother's son.

Drawing and art always appealed to Vera as a child; she was working on a special project at thirteen years of age. She was looking forward one particular day, when her father told her she was needed for potato picking, but she slipped off to school when she realized there were not many potatoes to pick. Plus, there was her father, two brothers, and sister to pick them; alas, her father arrived at the school gate and, despite her pleading for her painting class, he demanded she went with him. To this day Vera acknowledges the fact that her father could have picked the few potatoes she picked while he walked to the school and back. Vera was never known to paint after this.

One of the schoolteachers asked Vera if her father would provide her and her sisters with milk. They did and Vera loved to take the Miss Dawson's milk because there was always two chocolates on the plate on top of the basin.

Being in a hurry one day, Vera arrived home still eating a sweet. Her young sister, Rosie, asked where she had got the sweet, so Vera confessed, and Rosie started to scream. Her father scolded Vera and said in future she must bring the sweets home. She could not even eat one on the way but must take them both home and let Rosie choose which she wanted. If, for any reason, Vera could not go with the milk and Lilian, the eldest sister went, she ate both the sweets, and nothing was said.

At eleven years of age Vera took her exams for Beverley Academy. The teachers filled her with hope, assuring her by her class work she had a "walk over". The inspector came to the school and assured her she would be successful. The teachers asked Vera repeatedly if her results had come through and they never did. At least, Vera and her teachers never saw them and there would have been some notification even if she had failed, but then her father would have lost a good worker.

To Vera's great delight a photographer came to the school. A very unusual event, Vera saved her Saturday pennies carefully as she had never seen a photograph of herself. When they were developed, with great delight she was able to purchase one. She took it home and proudly showed it to her family, then placed it safely in her drawer. Every night, she opened the drawer to have a look at her precious photo. . . until one night it was missing. Disappointed and in great despair she ran crying to her mother.

"Have you seen my photograph?"

"Yes," she laughed. "I have sent it to your granny in Nottingham."

A heartbroken Vera never saw it again and never had a photo of her childhood.

Vera's brothers, as boys and later as young men, had a sense of humour that even their harsh father could not dispel. They put pram wheels and shafts on a rocking horse also put shafts on a bath chair, and shafts and wheels on a gaily painted swing boat discarded by the Fun Fair. They harnessed these up to the family's goats and set their three sisters, one in each, and led them round the Driffield Streets. It would be difficult today, but traffic was not so busy in those days.

At school the teacher asked if any pupil knew the "Last Rose of Summer". Vera said she did and was asked to sing it. As she began the other teachers told their pupils to put their pens down and listen. Her beautiful voice descended through the open windows. It was a voice that was rich, strong, and powerful; yet very sweet. Arriving home, she found the family gathered in the house and her sister, Lilian, seated at the piano, music book opened to the "Last Rose of Summer". Her sister, Rosie, had raced home and told of having to put their pens down and listen. So, Vera was told to sing. It's strange to say for a musical family how they chose to ignore Vera until now. This was the beginning of a singing career that was to span ten decades, and her voice was still as beautiful and sweet as ever. Never had there been a voice like it so admired by Christians and secular people alike all over the country. It would also be the last time she sang songs; something she refused to do for any audience or congregation.

"Let the word of Christ dwell in you richly in all wisdom; teaching and admonishing one another in psalms and hymns and spiritual songs, singing with grace in your hearts to the Lord." Colossians 3:16

"Speaking to yourselves in psalms and hymns and spiritual songs, singing and making melody in your heart to the Lord." Ephesians 5:19

A visiting preacher was coming to the Methodist Chapel for a special visit one afternoon. Vera was told to stay at home and look after Rosie. Their mother and Lilian went to the service. Her father was out and brothers were working. The Sisters had been alone for some time and were in the kitchen when they heard footsteps in their brothers' bedroom above. They were terrified as the workhouse was opposite and at times, they could have undesirable neighbours.

Vera opened the back door, got the yard brush, then opened front door for her little sister and told her to run and get help if she shouted. With the yard brush, Vera fearfully crept upstairs. She raised the brush and was about to rain blows down on her victim when she heard a yell.

"No! Don't! It's only me!"

It was her Mother.

Vera cried, "What are you doing in the lads' bedroom?"

Her mother replied, "Well, I felt unwell in the service and came home early and decided to see how you would react if someone got into the house."

Brokenhearted and distressed, Vera burst into tears.

Everard and William left school and began carting coal and goods to the shops, factories, and businesses in Driffield and the surrounding area. During the 1914-18 War, the other Carters were involved with Aerodrome work, which meant plenty of work in the Town. They carted coal and Coke from the railway station, took mail to the station every night from the post office, offal from the butcher's to the tip, and collected jumble for the various jumble sales, Took rock salt to Glover's Grocers and also carted for the chemist. Every Thursday afternoon, William took orders from Glover's Grocers to meet the carrier wagons coming in from the villages.

Lilian would go with Everard and fill the scuttles of coal on the cart for him to carry to their destination. Once or twice Vera had to go because Lilian was wanted somewhere else. She worked like a slave to have the scuttles filled ready for him to carry every time he returned to the cart; but all he did was find fault. When they arrived home he would say, "Hope you can come next time, Lil. You do it so much better."

Vera was so upset and wondered what she was doing wrong. She said, "Well, I had them ready every time you got back."

It was years later when her children told her that was the problem since he would have to wait for Lilian to fill them and was able to rest a bit.

Another job was cutting the various tennis courts in Driffield. The Parish Church, Weslyan Chapel, Primitive Chapel, and Baptist Church all had their own Courts. The Charters also cut the grass in the church yard; although, this was to be done by hand. Her father had special shoes made for the horses to cut the courts, so the hoof prints did no damage to the playing surface. Vera often went with her father to help and was very good at painting the white lines. She could keep them straight. But she was always sorry for the town's gentry, who played on the United Courts up Nafferton Road. Her father would leave the courts till the last minute which meant he was leaving as the players were arriving. Vera knew this was intentional since he liked speaking to the refined ladies. Even though she was so young, she realized how annoying this would be to the people involved so she watched him very carefully. One day she took the horse and cutter and cut it herself. She was away before the players arrived, but instead of being intensely grateful the treasurer said they would have to pay them less since a girl cut it on her own. Her father was not well pleased.

The Methodist Chapel meant everything to Vera's mother. She was seldom separated from her Methodist Hymn Book and seemed to receive much comfort in reading the good old hymns. She took her children with her to the services and because they were as good as gold, so she thought it would be easy to take little Vera with her. On taking their seats, Vera's eyes fell on the lovely needlework on the kneelers.

In a loud excited voice, she exclaimed, "Oh, Mammy, what a pretty bass." Awhile later in an equally loud voice she said, "Mammy, I've dropped my penny." As her great-grand mother kept a ladies school, this was a great embarrassment to Vera's Mother.

Chapter 3

A WORK FOR THE MASTER

FATHER HAD LEFT TO CUT the tennis court's ground, and, on his return, he saw some men erecting a large Tent in George Leason's field at Riverhead.

"What are you blokes doing?" he called good naturedly.

"We are evangelists." They replied.

"Real uns?" asked Father.

"Come and see. Service on Sunday," they answered.

"Oh, I can't come. I'm preaching."

"But it's not while eight o'clock when other Services are over."

Arthur was preaching at Hutton Cranswick and took Vera to sing a solo: "She Only Touched the Hem of His Garment". While going back to Driffield, he walked so quickly her feet hardly touched the ground. They went to the tent were George Ainsworth was preaching and never missed while it was there; this began their long association with the Christian Brethren.

"For we preach not ourselves, but Christ Jesus the Lord;" 2 Corinthians 4:5

Everard, William, and Lilian gave their hearts to the Lord at an evangelistic crusade held in Driffield. Previous to the tent coming when the speaker was Josiah Nix, Vera was concerned about the condition of her soul and was very much aware that she was lost and outside of Christ in the sight of a Holy God. When she was seven years of age, in Driffield Weslyan Chapel the preacher stressed the necessity of salvation and the need to give oneself to the Lord. Vera was under conviction and although only a child, her sins looked

23

as black as they could be and oh, how she longed to be forgiven. During the appeal at the close of the service, Vera went out. One of the counsellors came to her and asked, "Why are you here Vera?"

She replied, "I want to give my life to the Lord."

"Oh, you are too young," replied the counsellor. "Here. Sign the pledge." (the promise never to touch alcohol)

"But Jesus said, Suffer little children, and forbid them not, to come unto me; for of such is the kingdom of heaven" Matthew 19:14

At twelve years of age. Vera put her hand up when the appeal was given at another campaign. This time no one noticed her or if they did, chose to ignore her. When at a service of the Christian Brethren where Willie Clare had spoken, after the appeal was given Vera put up her hand once again. A Miss Priestley came to Vera and took her to Mr. Clare. He asked her why she wanted to become a Christian. Vera told him she had confessed to being a hell-deserving sinner, knew that the Lord had given His Life for her but had not been able to make a public witness of that profession.

"But sanctify the Lord God in your hearts: and *be* ready always to *give* an answer to every man that asketh you a reason of the hope that is in you with meekness and fear:" 1 Peter 3:15

Vera was later to make another witness when she was baptized in the sea.

"And as they went on *their* way, they came unto a certain water: and the eunuch said, See, *here is* water; what doth hinder me to be baptized? And Philip said, If thou believest with all thine heart, thou mayest. And he answered and said, I believe that Jesus Christ is the Son of God. And he commanded the chariot to stand still: and they went down into the water, both Philip and the eunuch; and he baptized him." Acts 8:36-38

Although Satan did not want to let Vera go, she now knew she had pleased her Lord and a very close walk it was between a sinner and her Saviour for over hundred years, to her dying day. Vera always doubted if anyone has had more prayers answered than she had.

Arthur sometimes took Vera to hold the horse's head while he was delivering on his carting jobs. On one occasion he was delivering goods to a large residential house in Driffield, being a particularly cold morning, the lady of the house asked them in for coffee. Her father always one to welcome the company of those ladies and gentlemen of the town—those of a class or two above his own—readily accepted. The lady insisted the horse was tethered, and the little girl came in too. When the kind hostess had gone to prepare the drinks, Vera said to her father, "I can't take coffee."

On appearing with the coffee, the lady asked if there was a problem.

Vera replied, "I can't take coffee."

The lady said she would make her a cup of tea.

Her father replied, "You drink what is put in front of you and that's that."

The poor little soul sat there trying to sip what to her was a revolting beverage.

When the cup was empty, Vera said, "Dad, I'm going to be sick." She made for the door failing to reach it and putting the contents of her stomach on the good lady's expensive carpet. Poor little Vera was covered with embarrassment and apologised profusely.

"Don't worry my dear it was your Father's fault he made you drink it."

Being the middle daughter, Vera often was left out of things at home. Her father, for some reason, had the three girls with him in the cart as he called at a house. The house holder used to it being only Arthur and a child to hold the horse, gave him two large juicy pears.

He got into the cart and promptly gave one to Lilian saying, "This is for you as you are the eldest." And he gave the other to Rosie saying, "You are the youngest."

It left Vera thinking she was invisible. This act of unkindness remained with Vera for the rest of her days, making her very careful to try and treat her own children in later years as fair as was possible.

At home, Arthur, on one of Lilian's birthdays, went across the room to her and gave her a shilling, then he went to Rosie, "Here's one for you. I missed your birthday."

Their mother, sweet timid soul that she usually was, quietly asked, "Where is Vera's? You missed her birthday, too?

"Oh, I only have two," he replied.

"Right." said her Mother, who never had any money of her own and always had to ask her husband for anything she needed.

She went upstairs and brought down a beautiful brooch, a George III 1817 Half Crown encased in a silver frame, which Arthur had bought her. "Then you shall have this, my dear."

It was always one of Vera's greatest treasures. Vera's mother always said Lilian and Rosie had taken after the Charter side and Vera the Thornhills which made father so partial.

Vera never wore make up of any kind when entertaining visitors. Her father put his arms around Lilian and Rosie and said these are my flowers, Lily and Rose.

Vera carried a lot of colour. Quick as a flash her mother went to Vera and said, "This is my flower, my Peony."

While still residing at No 1 Middle Street North, a young man called to say a donkey was walking down Eastgate on its own. Describing it to Vera, although only a child, she realised this particular donkey had a vicious streak and could bite or kick anyone and would not be easily caught. It was 7:30 a.m. and still dark. Only gas street lighting, but off she went after it. The donkey was passing the cake mill when she caught up with it, but she did not have a halter or anything to lead it with. A gentleman helped her turn it up Albion Street, two ladies turned it up Middle Street. Pedestrians on their way to work were very good stopping the wayward one from going down side streets. When nearly home, Vera asked a schoolboy if he would run on ahead, tell her father, and ask him to give her a turn into the yard. Both her father and Everard came out. By now it was daylight and her brother burst out laughing.

"What are you doing with this? It's not ours!" He exclaimed.

Father told the police sergeant, who lived next door, that it was at their home. The owner eventually came along from Nafferton and thanked Father profusely, then gave him ten shillings which Vera never received.

The Gospel Tent came for a second year and a campaign was held just before Vera's thirteenth birthday. George Ainsworth was again the evangelist. Vera's birthday was fast approaching, and she begged to be allowed some school friends home for a party. For once her parents agreed, and Lilian baked for the tea. It was agreed that three neighbour's daughters were to come. When everything was nearly ready there was a knock on the door and in walked George Ainsworth.

"You will stay for tea," said Father.

"Thank you, I will." Replied Mr. Ainsworth, not knowing of the party.

"Vera, go and tell your friends not to come." Stormed her father.

All the little girls plans, hopes, and dreams lay crushed in pieces. A heartbroken little girl had to go and knock on the doors of her friends and tell them not to come. Mr. Ainsworth finding out later what had happened and seeing Vera's tear-stained face gave her a shilling.

Mr. Ainsworth was not very tall and one evening was walking up to the tent with six very tall brethren, three on each side.

"Mr. Ainsworth," Vera's mother asked, "whatever did you feel like walking with those great men?"

"Mrs. Charter," the good man replied, "I felt like a sixpence between six penny worth of copper." That was when a penny was large in size.

Arthur sold his sixteen dairy cows in November 1915 and bought milk to sell on the milk rounds. The real reason is not known although it could be that Lily had five of a family and would have been unable to give him much assistance.

At thirteen years of age, Vera and her elder sister both had their own milk rounds. Her father was buying in milk to deliver to the customers. One evening, Vera and Lilian talked it over and decided as they had the fields the sensible thing to do would be to purchase a cow. Vera went to the market, at only thirteen years of age remember, and saw David Taylor, a well-known cattle dealer, who agreed to let Vera buy a cow and pay for it with the milk money bit by bit. Vera always maintained hire purchase was her idea.

David went to Vera's father, who was livid, but David got him to see reason and made the necessary arrangements. The real problem for young Vera was to keep the milk money from her father in order to save it for David. Vera vowed if she ever had a family of her own, they would never have anything unless the money was there to pay for it.

As I have said before Vera's mother was as a young woman renowned for her beauty. One day Arthur and David Taylor were having an argument which spilled out into the street. Voices were raised with Arthur shouting, "If everybody had their rights!"

He was cut off with David shouting back, "If everybody had their rights, Arthur, thou would have had my wife and I would have had thine"

The Charter family moved to No 6 Middle Street North, known as Church Farm, in 1924. While here, there was a mystery man in Driffield springing upon women on their own. It reached the national press. All round the town ladies were being escorted by their husbands or male friends, seldom going out alone. This went on for some considerable time. A sergeant at the police station one day asked if anyone has asked the Miss Charters if they had seen anything as they are about the town everyday with their milk rounds and go up most streets.

A policeman met Vera and asked if she had seen anything.

"Oh yes," she said. "I know who it is. It's Tommy."

Tommy was a Driffield man with learning difficulties who could not speak and just uttered guttural sounds but was totally harmless. He went about carrying a short piece of stick.

Vera said, "He goes up all the streets and alleys and when he hears anyone coming, he runs to where they are. And 'Uh! Uh! Uh!' he grunts. We just say, 'Hello, Tommy.' And he's satisfied, but it could be scary for anyone not knowing him."

The policeman said, "You could well be right." And that was the end of the Mystery Man in Driffield.

This same year George Leason purchased a large army hut and erected it in his large garden. This was known as Emmanuel Hall and the first Gospel Hall for Assembling of the Brethren in Driffield. The seats for the Hall were being made at Naylors at North End. One day the sirens sounded, and word spread quickly that there was a fire at Naylors. Willam, Vera's brother, and a friend, Jack Garner, realised the seats would be inside. They ran for all their worth and made their way inside. They were able to retrieve the complete and incomplete seats and get them to safety. John Naylor still charged them full price for the seats which would otherwise have gone up in flames.

For all her commitment to the Lord, giving her heart and life to Him, and accepting His offer of Salvation, and even with her strict upbringing, Vera soon realised the old nature was not easily put off.

One night there were some road works in the town—a row of red lights giving a warning up the side of them. The mischief in Vera wanted to put these lights out. Being young and full of fun she could not see the danger. She walked backwards and forwards, agonising over it. Her mischievous spirit striving for mastery. Eventually after deliberating on the matter for some time, her Lord gave her the victory and led her away all the lamps still brightly lit.

Chapter 4

EMMANUEL HALL

SOCIAL CONDITIONS WERE VERY DIFFERENT in Vera's young life and if people were not Christians, the majority were good, honest, hard-working folk. Most were connected to a place of worship. If they did not attend worship on the Lord's Day, then most likely they had been to Sunday school or sent their children to Sunday school.

There were very few cars; even if anyone owned one, they were slow and not suitable to travel long distances. Trains were not frequent. The speakers for Emmanuel Hall had to come on the train to stay the weekend at the homes of various members of the congregation They all had their favourites, and Mr. and Mrs. Somebody would have Mr. Soand-So but not Mr. Who Is It. So the elders had quite a job on their hands making everything pass off smoothly.

It meant a happy weekend for any children of the families, even if mothers and, in some cases, daughters were taken up with a lot of meals to organize. In many cases, children gave up their bedrooms for a couple of nights.

One delight of the Charter Family was the Saturday night Open Air Service in the Market Place. Vera's brother, William, was extremely strong despite his wiry frame. He could hold all four spark plugs on a Tractor when it was running, and he would carry the harmonium down on his shoulder. The visiting preacher for the weekend would speak. Lilian played the harmonium and Vera would sing a solo. One Monday Vera was tenting their cows up Allotment Lane when one of the men on the allotments called to her.

"I heard you singing on Saturday night."

"Oh, were you at the open air meeting?" she replied.

"No, I was up here."

Vera said, "You could not hear me all that distance."

"I could. I said to the other lads, 'That's Miss Charter singing'."

He told her the hymn she had sung. She had a truly remarkable voice, powerful yet sweet and melodious. At one Open Air Meeting a man who was much the worse for drink, approached the circle and listened to the speaker for a few minutes then threw some coins into the middle. Quick as a flash Lilian sprang from the organ, scooped up the money, and ran through the crowd to him, saying, "Here! Here! Take this. It's not your money we want; it's you."

Next Saturday evening he arrived at the Open Air Meeting stone cold sober, cleanly shaven, and smartly dressed saying, "Where's the young lady that wants me."

It took a long while for Lilian to live that one down.

Vera's mother was never a strong woman—a rather sad quiet lady.

When her second son, William, arrived he was a twin. Both were born alive, although delicate, it was known that one would survive, but the other would not. They decided to name one John after Lily's father and also after the beloved brother, who had died as a child. The other was named William after Arthur's father. The birth was in Driffield, and as mentioned before in a town full of Arthur's relatives. Lily, although too frail and weak with the birth to do or say anything, heard one of the family say, "Name that one John because it won't live."

It was a great sadness to her burying not only her baby but also her father's name.

At Vera's birth Lily wanted to name her Helen, a name she loved, but Arthur said, "No, we are not having any 'hells' in this House."

When the family were grown, Everard was a beautiful sign writer, not as a business—just something he was good at. He wrote his name on the side of his cart.

Lily was watching him taking his cart out of the yard and exclaimed, "Well I never. I could not have Helen, and we have a son E.L Charter, a daughter L Charter, and the youngest Rosalind Rachel."

Rosalind was born prematurely and was always delicate. When preachers were staying at the family home, Vera would be enthralled with a debate or musings on the Scriptures. When the summons would come about eight o clock, she was told, "Vera, take Rosie to bed."

This not just to take her upstairs, but Vera had to stay with her. That was the end of her entertaining evening. She never knew why it was always her and no one else had to take Rosie to bed.

Mr. George Corson and Mr. Parkin from Leeds, two businessmen of some standing, were staying at the Charters' home. Mr. Corson preached at the weekend meetings.

The first time they came Mr. Corson went up to little Rosie and asked, "What is your name?"

"Rosie," was the reply.

"Oh," he said. "I have a little Daisy at home."

The next few visits Arthur would say, "And how is little Daisy?"

"Oh, very well, thank you," was the reply.

One day Mr. Parkin took Arthur to one side and whispered, "Do you not know the little Daisy he spoke about is Mr. Corson's wife?"

After the end of the weekend meetings, Vera would carefully wash her stockings—as they were in very short supply during and after the war—fold them, place them in a drawer ready for the next weekend, and would go bare legged during the week. It was not unusual for her to go to her drawer the next weekend and find the stockings missing; however well she managed to hide them, and the usual cry went up, "Has anyone seen my stockings?"

Knowing well it was her mother or Lilian who wore theirs all the week laddered them and saw fit to take hers.

Vera took her first Sunday school class when she was thirteen years of age. One small boy in her class was a terror, misbehaving all the time. He refused to accept any form of authority. One day Vera was walking down the town and met him. A pleasant enough lad, he stopped for a word.

Vera asked him why he behaved so badly in Sunday School.

"Do you realise the Lord is watching you? He loves you and wants you to love and trust Him. One day you will have to stand before the Lord and tell Him why you were so naughty, and He will ask why you didn't accept Him and His love. It is your decision at the moment if you want to go to Heaven or Hell but one day you will stand before the Lord and as you don't accept him now, He will not accept you then. As well as the Lord, you are upsetting me, your teacher, and your classmates, who are eager to learn. Why are you doing this?"

The lad kept coming to Sunday school and was no more trouble. His mother stopped Vera one day and remarked about her son and the change in his behaviour; he was so good now.

Vera had many friends she met through Emmanuel Hall. One, who was very dear to her, was Millie Garner. Her and her husband had the Fish and Chip Shop near Cross Hill. Jack passed away while young. Millie, before he passed away was going through a time of illness. Nothing seemed to do her any good. Vera's father had one of the electrical medical coils which ran off a battery. There was a hand grip for each hand and like a dipstick you gradually pressed down to allow more current to pass into the patient. Millie could take a fair amount of this and owned it was doing her a lot of good. Shortly after on a visit to the doctor, Millie discovered she was expecting and went on to have a very healthy baby. She said she was not the least bit surprised when he grew up to be an electrician.

Mr. George Bradford from Bradford was the visiting preacher one weekend. At the tea table in the company of the speaker, Lily, Vera's mother, said she thought there must have been a sermon in a magazine or a penny sermon out recently on Naaman as in 2 Kings 5:1-27. The last three speakers had all taken him as their subject. Shortly after the speaker asked to be excused from the table, he was ages in the room where they went for a quiet time before going to the service. He was a very able speaker but the family at home after the service said they had never heard him speak worse and wondered what could have been the matter.

Lily said, "I think we were going to get Naaman again."

The Burnham brothers came to take services at Emmanuel Hall. They were evangelists and pen manufacturers from 1920 until 1960. The pens they made are now collector's items—being British made and of exceptional quality and some having gold nibs and fittings and command high prices.

On one visit Bert went into the room to pray and prepare for the service. The time went on and on. The family all set off for the meeting, all but Vera. She waited and waited, eventually she knocked on the door, but nothing happened. So she gently opened it and, looking in, saw him fast asleep on the settee. Vera woke him.

Not in the least grateful, he was annoyed at being found out, however when they set off for the service, Bert said, "Am I walking too fast for you Vera?"

To which she replied, "No."

"Then can we walk a little faster?" he exclaimed.

One evening Bert infuriated Lily when he said from the pulpit, he had never had a square meal since he came to Driffield, although she left the baking of cakes and pastries to her daughters, her dinners and meals were quite something. Also, her bread was wonderful—those delicious farmhouse loaves crusty on the outside but so soft inside.

When remonstrating with Bert at supper time he said, "Well, how can you have a square meal off a round plate?"

A nurse, who lived between Driffield and Nafferton and worked at the hospital, had started to attend the meetings at Emmanuel Hall, but said she was very nervous going back in the dark alone. She asked if someone would see her home. Either Everard or William would see her safely back until one night Vera and Lilian were down the town delivering milk when they heard peals of mirth coming from a seat in the marketplace.

On closer investigation they saw the nurse seated splitting her sides with laughter and a crowd of lads round her. So needless to say, at the next meeting she asked who was going to see her home, Lilian and Vera took her, unfortunately she lost some of her enthusiasm for the meetings.

Some weekends a group of young men would come to Driffield to help establish the meetings at Emmanuel Hall. There was Albert Lancaster from Bradford who endeared himself to all and there was never a shortage of offers of places for him to go and stay. One year he sent the three Charter girls a handkerchief each for Christmas. These were not used for many years but treasured. Stanley Ward, Harry and John Green, Alfie, Ken and Leslie Young, all from Hull, were great help to the fledgling meeting and were morale boosters to the Charter family. Leslie Elvidge, who had a great command of the Scriptures, and his mother came regularly to assist.

Mr. King and Stanley Douglas Bowler came from Nottingham. They provided much needed help and inspiration to the young members of the Charter family.

Mr. King was a well-known fruit merchant aptly named in Nottingham as the Banana King. On one of his visits he said next time he came he would teach them a new chorus.

Vera said, "I know what that will be."

"What will it be?" asked Mr. King.

"By and by, we'll see the King," was the reply.

Father was annoyed but Mr. King loved her joke.

After the move to No 6 Middle Street North, Vera was cleaning the front bedroom were the speakers slept. Having done the ceiling with whitewash, which was lime and water in those days, and being very careful as always, Vera was always a tidy worker. Not having any drips or drops where they should not be, she had finished and was called away for a few minutes. On returning she could not believe her eyes whitewash was pouring across the window, up the wall, across the floor.

"Mother!" Vera called. "Who's been in here?"

"I have," her Mother replied. "You must let the neighbours see that you are cleaning."

It took Vera longer to clear up the mess than it had to do the painting. The following is a letter received from the above mentioned Stanley Douglas Bowler, in which he mentions Sir Jessie Boot the founder of Boots Chemists.

West Bridgeford,

Notts.

July 11th 1928

Dear Friends.

At last I am writing you in reply to the letter for which very many thanks.

Isn't the weather glorious? Do hope you like this for the holidays. Bye the bye we, that is Mother, Father, my younger brother and two cousins, who are over on holiday from Vancouver, and myself are going to Filey for our holidays commencing on 11th August. My brother and I most probably push or motor cycling (depends on whether my old Motor Cycle will go without being carried) If we do this we shall I think go via Hull and from there to Driffield, so we shall hope to have a look at you all – unless you have come to Nottingham for the day.

Well I wonder how the Meetings (Emmanuel Hall) are going on and the Baptisms? Neither Father or I will ever forget the great times we had when we were there, the Meetings, the People and everything in general.

Most probably Mr. C. H. King has told you all about the Parade Halls Young Peoples Meeting and what a great success it was – there were about fifteen or more Saved during the season and Mr. King is by letters keeping in touch with all of them until we recommence with a reunion tea in September.

During part of the winter we also had a Saturday night class for the elder ones were singing took part of the time. This happy band has now developed into a Tract Band which goes every Saturday into outlying villages near enough so as not to be expensive, yet far enough away to feel your house is not round the corner, if you can understand my meaning.

I suppose you know the Royal Agricultural Show is being held in Nottingham this week, and that the King and Queen opened the new University to which Sir Jesse Boot has given a million pounds. Nottingham is of course decked up to the eyes in red, white and blue and looks right fine. His Majesty is coming to Kirby today and each teacher has to march his class for a mile down the road in order that the children have a good view of the Royal pair.

Well the other teachers will be here very soon and I have four sets of marking to do so I guess I had better get on with it. If you have a spare five minutes sit down and write a few lines in the same way as I have done, if its only half as long as this scrappy note it will awaken my thoughts of some very good people in Driffield.

Kindly remember me to your Mother and Father,

With kindest regards and Christian Greetings,
Your Sincere Friend
Stanley Douglas Bowler

Chapter 5

LIFE IN DRIFFIELD

LILIAN AND VERA WERE WALKING down the street one day with Jack, a large dog of theirs which they had been allowed to keep. Usually when they became really fond of a donkey or a dog they would come home and find it missing. Their father would have traded it to some passing gypsies, leaving his family broken hearted. The sisters had their dog on a lead when they met a rather fashionable lady with a small yappy dog not secured. It rushed across the road and seized Jack by the throat. Vera clicked the wee one by the scruff of its neck and sent it flying back across the road.

"My dog! Oh, my dog!" Screamed the lady. "You have killed it."

But the dog got on its feet and scurried back to her as fast as it could none the worse for its flying lesson.

Arthur believed all his family should stay at home. He made them promise that his daughters would not have anything to with boyfriends and his sons would not have anything to do with girlfriends—until they were twenty-one. That is all, but Vera, who refused to make such a promise. Her father had a whistle and if as children they were playing in the street and he whistled that meant they had to go home, which usually meant he had seen them having a good time. This he continued in later life and if the daughters were speaking to a man or the sons to a lady in the street, and he saw them, he would whistle for them to come. Again, they all went running home except Vera. Indeed, he did take his belt off to her once, but Everard got between and for once put his foot down.

Harry and John Green came one weekend to help with the meetings and each had just purchased lovely gleaming motor bikes. They asked the girls if they would like a spin. Lilian was scared but they managed to avoid Father and there was nothing in it. Harry and John were just like brothers to them.

Lilian and Vera did attend night classes. Lilian was very good at mental arithmetic—something that stayed with her to her dying day. In school, Vera excelled in learning; her lecturer went to see her father, to know if he would allow her to go to Hull Technical College. Her Father refused.

"It's a case of protecting her morals." Which did not seem to apply when he made the sisters do their milk rounds in the town in the dark.

After hearing Vera sing on the marketplace on a Saturday night, Mr. Longbottom, who had the sweet and mineral water factories in Driffield, and Mr. Sammy Gibson, who owned much property in the town, went to see Arthur about sending Vera to have her voice trained. Once again, her father refused.

Many of the townsfolk cared deeply for Vera; she was very popular chiefly because of her beautiful singing. One jeweler stopped her father in the street and said he had a special watch (and to) come into the shop. He asked her father if he would send his daughter in because he would like to give it to her.

"I'll send Lilian in then."

"No, it's not for Lilian. It's for Vera."

Their father was bound to tell Vera as he knew she would eventually see the jeweler and find out. How she loved that watch. Some considerable time later she lost it as she took the cows back to the field from milking. It was one thing Vera never did. She never milked the cows. The rest of the family did, even her mother. So, it was her job usually to bring the cows in and take them back to the field. William found the watch a year later. He cleared the dirt from it, wound it up, and it ticked merrily away. Another treasure she had was a star brooch given her by the same jeweler.

Foot-and-mouth disease came to Driffield. The family were in the unenviable position of having house and buildings in the town and fields on the outskirts. The cows had to be brought to the buildings twice a day for milking and then returned to the pastures. A permit had to be obtained to move the animals. Bonfires of cattle were blazing all round which had fallen prey to the dreaded disease. Much prayer was offered both by the family and their friends and the Lord kept His promise.

". . . neither shall any plaque come nigh thy dwelling." Psalm 91:10.

One of Vera's early recollections was of her father and his brother, John, having a discussion one day. Both sat with long faces, deep in conversation. It was Uncle John who had a grocers shop in Victoria Road. John was recalling something that had troubled him for many years, and he had not wanted to divulge it until now, when he could bear it no longer. As a boy, he was thirsty during the night. He went downstairs for a drink of water and saw his father, William Charter, with a large box that cheeses came in. It was full of sovereigns, which their father appeared to be counting. At first his father was so occupied he did not see him, but when he did, he ordered him back to bed. It troubled John and he wondered for years what happened to those coins. Just where did they go? Vera often wondered if John got his drink of water.

Vera had two great friends at school. Enid Thompson lived in Victoria Road and was head and shoulders taller than any of the other girls. Vera and Enid always sat together for lessons when this was possible. When the new headmistress, Miss Tunnicliffe, who was small, came to the school she took one look at Enid and said, "Are all the girls as tall as you?"

Evelyn Knaggs was another great friend. She later married and was then called Backhouse and lived in King Street. It was a friendship that lasted for many years. They met when Evelyn attended the meetings in Emmanuel Hall with her mother. Vera, who had not many possession's, always kept some small gifts given to her by Evelyn.

A girl from the country by the name of Sarah Towse came to live in the town. She gave Vera's brothers great delight to hear her beautiful Yorkshire dialect. They made sure they were in the house, if at all possible, whenever she called. Vera was not good at rising in the morning.

Sarah would knock at the door and when it was opened would say, "Is Vera riddy?"

"Hes she getten her beats on yit."

The brothers loved it.

Vera and Lilian got into sore trouble with father over an incident at Emmanuel Hall. Mr. Maidens, an elderly gentleman from Driffield, read the Scriptures during the morning meeting. He read from Matthew 26:6–3, about the woman with the alabaster box of precious ointment and her pouring it over the Lords head. At the end of verse seven it says, "**as he was sat *at meat*,**"; the beginning of verse eight says, "**But when the disciples saw *it*, they had indignation**"; the dear old gentleman read, "as he sat at meat, the disciples were filled with indigestion."

Vera was at one end of the seat and Lilian at the other; they just went into a fit of giggles the idea of being sat at meat and being filled with indigestion. The problem was their father was seated in the middle of the seat and could feel the seat shaking from the girls laughing. When they got home, father demanded to know what they had been laughing at They told him, and he laughed too and admitted he had never heard it. But mother ever one to see problems told them they must apologise to Mr. Maidens because someone may cause trouble. When the gentleman came for his milk, they said they were sorry for laughing, but did he realise he had made a mistake? They told him what he had said. He had not realised and laughed too, then said, "Thank you very much for telling me. Mrs. Botterill came to me after the meeting and said, 'Did you know the Charter girls were laughing at you this morning?'"

Outings and holidays were virtually unknown to the family. One occasion, which gave the family great delight, was when the Walton Street

Assembly in Hull invited the Driffield young folk to Beverley Westwood for the afternoon. They enjoyed games and a picnic, which no doubt it caused their parents grief, but they could not stop it since the sons were grown up now. Everard, being some ten years older than Vera, had a great time with the Young family, Green family, Stanley Ward and Leslie Elvidge, and all the Walton Street young folk. Lilian and Vera were invited to Nottingham to stay with their aunts and uncles for a holiday. Lilian was allowed to go but Vera was told that there were not enough funds for both of them.

The next year Vera asked her father who, was not the best businessman in the world, if she could collect the money owing to him on outstanding bills and save the money for her fare to Nottingham. She was told she could but only if she collected and saved enough to take Lilian too. Vera being astute went round the debtors homes and workplaces and asked them how much they could afford to give her each week off their accounts to pay their debts. Some could not pay very much but all were pleased to be able to get their outstanding bills cut down and be faced with the prospect that they would eventually get them cleared. Vera faithfully went on her rounds every week and marked down carefully what was paid. The folk were delighted to be getting out of debt, and Vera was getting nearer her holiday. As the pennies mounted up, she would see a nice hat or article of clothing to purchase for her holiday. But when she arrived home, she had to go back and get one for her sister, even though Lilian was five years older.

A Mrs. Berryman lived in the town and told Arthur she had purchased a suit that did not fit her. She asked if he would send Vera to try it on. Upon arriving, Vera saw it was a dress and coat in a rich wine colour which fitted her perfectly—her first designer outfit!

At the same time the family were leading jumble for a sale at the Wesleyan Chapel. Mrs. Temple who operated a high class store in town called Vera to her stall and produced a long white Boa, which when she got it home and tried it on with her suit, it reached right down to the hem. Miss Poole had a milliners shop in Middle Street South. Vera told her about the outfit and asked if she had a hat to match. She produced a large navy one which suited Vera very well.

Miss Poole said, "Wait a minute." She kindly placed a large white rose at the side.

With her outfit complete, Vera was thrilled and walking on air. Lilian was invited to Leeds for the annual Brethren Conference on the Saturday. Vera's father told her to take Lilian's milk round so she could get ready to go and catch the train, as she was coming up Exchange Street. Vera saw Lilian walk across the end going down Middle Street to the station dressed in Vera's new outfit. Vera broke down and cried in despair realising most of the brethren she knew would be there and would now think her beautiful outfit was one of Lilian's cast offs. Not only that, but Lilian never took care of her clothes and was going with a white fur on a steam train.

Mark Wicks and Stanley Douglas Bowler from Nottingham and Norman Tomlin, who wrote the much loved tune, "Supremacy", in the Believers Hymn Book, came to stay in Driffield to help with the work at Emmanuel Hall. Mr. King, previously as mentioned before he was much loved by the family, announced one morning that they were going to the seaside at Bridlington and they would like the family to go with them. This caused great excitement.

Arthur said, "That's fine. Vera can stay and take the milk out."

"Oh no," replied Mr. King, sitting down. "If Vera can't go, no one will."

"Alright. Get your milk out first, then," said Father.

"Can we help?" asked the young men.

So, Stanley Douglas Bowler carried Vera's milk pail, so she was able to go too.

In the 1920s, men were gentlemen and ladies were gracious; everyone knew their manners. Lilian was walking down the town when she met the bank manager riding his bicycle. He raised his bowler hat and in so doing it slipped from his grasp and fell to the floor. Poor Lilian did not know what to do. Ought she to pick it up? Quickly she thought the kindest thing to do was to hurry on as though she had not seen.

Vera's uncle had a footpath across his farm which caused him problems. Town folk had the habit of taking a wider and wider path across the fields. He found a very unpleasant way of dealing with the annoyance. One morning his son went and tarred all the stiles. About lunch time Vera's mother wondered what was the matter. All the ladies were walking sideways down the street in their beautiful long dresses with their husbands trying to shield them. It was only next day at school they learned that the ladies had sat on the stiles as they climbed over them.

For the rest of his life his son was known as "Tarry Robson!" The son went on to live years later on a farm at Sawdon near Scarborough, a cattle dealer from Great Edstone near Kirkbymoorside. Lorne Wilkinson received a call to see him about some calves. Upon arriving, Albert's second wife came bowing and scraping, welcoming Lorne into their home. Taking him into the lounge and seating him in a comfortable chair, Lorne in his working clothes was lapping up all the attention with just a little touch of embarrassment. Out came the family silver and china cups and saucers; dainty sweetmeats were placed before him peppered with, "Are you alright? Are you comfortable?"

The lady was going to a lot of trouble to please her guest after a lot more bowing and curtseying. Albert could stand it no longer.

"Whatever is the matter with you, woman? It's only Lorne."

"Lorne!" she stammered. "I thought you said it was Lord Wilkinson!"

Lilian had a love for horses but once received a stern reprimand from her mother. There were four horses in a carriage coming through Driffield. When the horses were startled and bolted, they were dashing madly down the main street totally out of control, people were fleeing left and right. As they came thundering past, Lilian, slightly built only five feet two, ran out and grabbed hold of one of the traces. This slowed them down until several men raced to her assistance and got them stopped. Her daring feat got her a mention in the local paper. All Lilian could say was "poor things they might have been killed."

Vera never loved horses only Diddy, who was part horse and part donkey. Diddy had a will of her own. It took two men to catch her with a rope and they had to be quick. Vera started to give her cow-cake nuts as a treat, and she could eventually catch her on her own. The family bought Diddy at Driffield. She moved to Barmston with them, and she was very fast—able to do twelve miles an hour.

The brothers and sisters all played the piano, but Lilian was generally the accepted accompanist. She regularly accompanied her two brothers when they played their violins. One Lord's Day evening after the service at Emanuel Hall, friends had gathered as usual in the Charter home for supper and a sing of the good old Gospel Hymns around the piano. It was summertime. The sash windows were pushed open and the balmy air floating in. The melodies floating out into the ears of passer's by. The speakers from Emmanuel Hall Mr. Parkin and Mr. George Corson, a businessman from Leeds, were staying the weekend.

There was a knock at the door and Vera's father went to open it. A man pushed past him—a man of gentlemanly bearing, very well dressed; he sat down and began to take his boots and socks off.

"Just a minute, brother." said Arthur "You can't stay here we're full up."

It was obvious by his speech and actions he was not well mentally. In the course of the evening the brothers and sisters could not help giggling. After supper, their father managed to persuade him to leave.

"Do not laugh at this man. He has been a godly man in his time. Something has happened to turn his mind," said Mr. Parkin.

Arthur said to Mr. Parkin and Mr. Corson, "Don't worry. You gentlemen were so kind and considerate to him, I told him you were going to Leeds on the train in the morning so he will be waiting so he can travel with you."

When the family arrived at Driffield Station to see them off, Mr. Parkin went for a paper when who should be approaching him in the opposite direction but the aforesaid gentleman. Mr. Parkin saw him and pulled up his coat collar, turning his face away, much to the amusement of the Charter Family. When Mr. Parkin returned with his paper, their father said, "Steady, brother, steady. He has been a godly brother in his time."

One Lord's Day evening, when supper was over and the family and friends were gathered around the organ, a knock came at the door. When Arthur opened it, a tramp stood there. Not an unusual sight in Driffield.

"I heard a violin playing," he said. "May I come in and play it"

Quite a shock to father, but nothing deterred he invited him in. He was immediately passed a violin. The man tuned it, put it under his chin, and the most beautiful and melodious music issued forth. It transported the listeners to another realm. Taking the violin from his chin he undid the bow, put the horsehair part under the strings, tightened up the bow again, and commenced playing. What sounded was like the sweetest canary singing any one had ever heard.

What a wonderful evening the family had one they never forgot. On leaving the tramp asked if he could borrow the violin while in Driffield so he could make himself some money. The family, although well aware of the risk, agreed and that was the last they saw of tramp and violin. They only hoped he made a living through playing the instrument and did not sell it to obtain money for alcohol, but for the rest of their days wondered who they had entertained and who had entertained them.

The family had gathered for a meal when the postman delivered a very small parcel. "Oooh, someone's got married and sent us some cake," was the general comment. "Who can it be?" they queried and crowded around.

"It's addressed to Dad!" someone exclaimed.

It was passed to their father. "O, you curious lot!" he yelled, opened the door of a tall cupboard, and threw it onto the top shelf where it landed amongst the glassware. Eventually spring came. Vera was cleaning out the cupboard when she came across the tiny box.

"Oh, that box of wedding cake. Someone should have had a present." she said to her mother.

"Open it," her mother replied.

When she did it was a box of pills father had sent for and forgotten about. These were kept out of sight until all the family where in for a meal.

Vera calmly announced, "You remember the box of wedding cake Dad threw to the top of the cupboard? Well here it is."

And with great glee showed them the box of pills.

"Father didn't need them very badly, did he?" Vera could hardly be heard for the peals of mirth that issued forth.

At bedtime Vera used to hang out of the window of her sisters' bedroom talking to them when a weird sound floated over Driffield for several evenings. It was eerie and only began at dusk; most of the townsfolk thought it was a ghost. It seemed as if that the sound was coming from the church. Rumours began that the church was haunted. One night, Vera was looking out of the window when she saw a screech owl fly over in the direction of the church. As it neared the church, the noise started up, and Vera realised that the owl had a nest of young ones. When the owls neared the church with food the young ones set up this weird noise. Being in the top of the church it carried all over the town since there was little traffic to drown the sound.

Being very resourceful, Vera was sorry for her mother having to light the fire on a morning with damp sticks and seeing her search around the yard for bits of wood to get it going filled her with dismay. So every time Vera went to the fields with the cows in the summer time she brought branches back, She broke them up and made them into bundles about the size of the grate, the thin pieces at the bottom and thicker towards the top. She then tied them with Massey Harris binder band later to be called baler twine. Vera was close to her brother, Everard, and asked him where she could hide them until winter. He found a hay rack in a shed not in use and put some loose hay at the front to conceal them. Vera made a hundred and fifty bundles one a day for the winter.

When the cold damp days arrived, Vera came in tired one evening and went to her store of carefully prepared sticks to take one in for her mother for morning, only to find not one bundle remained. Vera went into the house in tears.

"What have you done with my winter supply of sticks?" she cried.

Her mother turned round with a grin on her face. "Oh, I found them and used them to pop up the fire when your dad wanted a cup of tea."—such was her devotion to her husband. It over came any loyalty to her children. It was particularly harrowing for Vera as her dad claimed to be an invalid and spent most of his time sitting in front of the fire or in bed.

In later years, her mother said how she would love a large roll of beef at hay time, something to slice at when the family came in hungry from the fields. When hay time arrived, Vera biked to the butcher's and brought home this much prized roll. Being busy with the crops, and fitting in the caring for the sheep and cows in between, Vera forgot about the roll until one evening her mother said how she would love a large roll of beef to cut into when they came in hungry.

"Well," Vera said. "I got you one."

"Oh, I've used that."

Vera asked her brothers and sisters. "Have you had any of that big roll of beef I got Mam?"

"No, we haven't." They all answered.

So approaching, her mother she said, "Mam, where's that roll of beef I got you?"

"Oh, I cooked that for your dad. He likes a bit of beef."

He liked meat so much that when the family went in for dinner their mother would start carving whatever meat it was, passing their father his first. She would serve everyone then look up and say, "Oh, I haven't given your father any meat."

She would immediately reach up and take the meat off her and Vera's plates and put it on her husband's. This began happening all too often. So Vera paid particular attention and saw her father's plate complete with meat set down before him.

Immediately, he rolled it up and popped it into his mouth and virtually swallowed it whole. Vera's mother continued to serve and as usual cried out. "Oh, I haven't given your father any meat."

He was then given the meat as usual off her own and Vera's plates. Vera dare not say anything but told Everard to keep a watch. When the same procedure was repeated another day and the "Oh, I haven't given your father any meat."

Everard shouted out, "Yes, you have! He's eaten it!"

Vera said, "Yes, and he's been eating my meat for a long time and I'm sick of it especially when I'm doing his work."

Their father pushed his chair back and went upstairs to bed.

"You shouldn't have said anything. You have upset your father." Mother replied.

Vera was cutting turnips for the cows. She was down to the last scuttle full when Lilian rushed up and said, "Let me give you a turn."

"No, I'm alright. I've nearly finished." Vera replied at which she was pushed out of the way.

Lilian picked up the scuttle and had just gone a yard or two when her father and Everard came round the corner. "Well done, Lilian, well done." It was no accident her timing was perfect.

Going onto Frosts, the butcher, and waiting in the queue, Vera noticed her maiden aunt came in behind her. She was a dressmaker of some self-importance.

Mr. Frost looked up and said, "What can I get for you Miss Charter?"

Vera's aunt stepped forward so dignified, but he said "Not you. I meant my Miss Charter." Vera was delighted.

A friend, Stanley Ward of Hull, was marrying Grace Taylor. The family had been invited to the wedding. Vera found a very nice dress and coat and altered the coat to the season's style. She cut up an old coat and put a piece round on the bottom and decorated collar and cuffs with the same material. She was thrilled when she found a hat to go with it. A friend in a shop in Driffield got her a large flower to go on the side. She bought a present and was all ready for the big day. On the morning after, rushing with her milk round, she was told by her father that she had to take Lilian's milk round. When she arrived home her brothers and sisters had left in the car, which meant she could not go. When they arrived home, Vera was in for a bigger shock. Lilian was again wearing the outfit Vera had prepared.

When Vera protested that she could never wear it as everyone would think it was Lilian's cast off, Lilian said she had not found anything to wear. It was easy since she was father's favourite not to go to any trouble and then get him to keep Vera at home and use her outfit.

A real heartache to the family was that Vera's father had no affection for anything and they dreaded the gypsies coming into the area. He would sell or swap anything with them. They could come home from the fields and find a well-loved dog or donkey or horse had been swapped. Not only was a beloved pet gone but he never was good at business and had usually swapped or sold it for something far inferior.

Chapter 6

A MOVE TO BARMSTON

THE FAMILY MOVED IN APRIL 1930 when Vera was nineteen years old to Elm Tree Farm, Barmston, which was on the coast between Bridlington and Hull. They had more land with the farm and being close to the seaside, they were also able to take paying guests as they were then known.

When moving from Driffield to Barmston, Vera's brother, William, had a horse and rulley (a flat farm cart) and cousin Albert Robson from Wansford had two horses and a rulley. Vera had a horse and rulley. William and Albert made excellent progress. Vera was a bit behind having a sectional shed on which after a while with the motion the sections began to slide, and Vera had to stop. While pondering what to do the police superintendent's son passed in a car. Seeing she was having problems, he stopped and wanted to know if he could help. Vera told him William was ahead, would he go and ask him to come back.

As previously stated, although William was tall and thin, he was very strong; he could hold four plugs in a tractor while the engine was running. Now why anyone would want to do that is beyond the imagination, but then most young lads want to be stronger than each other. The superintendent's son did better than that. He waited until William secured his horse and he brought William back in the car. The load was straightened, and the travelers were on their way. Vera had packed eggs and bacon, a frying pan, and kettle to have a hot meal. When they arrived after their fourteen mile journey—with horse and cart remember—Vera found the bag with the food and utensils and went to prepare. Alas, when unpacking, there was no frying pan. Her mother had taken it out to cook her father's breakfast. So, they had to make do with cups of tea.

In the summer, the brothers and sisters loved to walk up to the sea for a swim or paddle, but with Vera's jobs on the farm and preparing and caring for the paying guests Vera had not many spare evenings.

The farm was owned by the Wickham Boyntons of the Burton Agnes Estate. Most of the land belonging to Elm Tree Farm was about three quarters of a mile away off the Bridlington to Hull road. One day the hunt was out, and Vera arrived at the sheds to do some work when a gentleman came round the buildings covered in blood. Vera took him to a shed and sat him on some hay, cleaned him up, and tended his injuries as best she could with what was available. He explained his horse had thrown him. Vera wanted to go for an ambulance, but he refused saying he was now well enough to ride. As he was leaving, he thanked Vera profusely and gave her a small card which she slipped into her pocket, thereby forgetting all about it; only remembering it when she arrived home. She took it out and it was a business card with his name and address on it: Lord Middleton.

Vera enjoyed having the paying guests; although, the work was tiring especially as there was also more work to do on the farm, with it being a larger acreage than Driffield.

Most of the visitors were splendid though there where odd ones that really tried Vera's patience. A wealthy couple with the BOCM animal food firm came for the weekend from Hull. The husband came in on the Monday morning before they went home.

"Can I borrow a gun?"

No objections were raised and eventually he came in with some rabbits; meanwhile, his wife said she was going for a walk and in she came with a basket of mushrooms from the fields. She asked for a sack and went into the orchard and filled it with fallen apples. These were all put into their car. Then the wife came running back.

"Oh, can you spare me a dozen eggs?"—which were supplied though more consternation when she said, "Goodbye. See you again next week."

They got in the car without paying. Vera was livid saying all their profits had gone, in that car.

Her father said, "You wanted to take paying guests so you must expect it."

He always had a soft spot for wealthy people. Weekend after weekend the couple came and whatever was in season was pulled or shot and taken back to Hull. Vera could stand no more so on the Friday before they arrived, she hid the guns, she went down the orchard and picked all the fallen apples, went into the fields and picked whatever mushrooms she could find. Come the Monday morning the husband asked for the gun.

Vera said, "Oh, it doesn't seem to be here."

The wife went into the fields and came back with a few pathetic mushrooms; she went into the orchard and came back with no apples. As she was leaving, she said "Oh, I've forgot the eggs."

So Vera went for them and said, "These are one shilling a dozen." Needless to say, they never had their visitors from Hull again.

The brothers and sisters had some great times as the young folk from the Hull, Bradford, and Leeds Brethren Assemblies were beginning to get cars and motor bikes. It was a lovely ride to Barmston with its sea, sand bracing air, and the home baked food at the farm. Now living at Barmston much thought was given by the family as to where to go to worship. For some time, they continued to travel to Driffield, though this was not always expedient as farmers operating a mainly stock farm with no outside help. A calving cow or lambing sheep could make all the difference being able to attend a service or not. The brothers and sisters did all possible to be present at the morning meeting—so important to gather in the Lord's name and break bread as their

Lord ordained in His Word they should: **"this do in remembrance of me."**
Luke 22:19

When taking visitors, it was not always possible to travel for the evening service. So the family would attend the village chapel service. The brothers and sisters retained their musical talent and would take musical evenings to the chapels at the local villages Skipsea, Ulrome, Beeford, Bempton, and Reighton, etc. The brothers took their violins and cello; Vera and Rosalind sang solos and duets; the sisters all said recitations; Everard, William, Vera, and Rosalind sang quartets and Lilian played the organ or piano for them. These evenings were much appreciated and remembered by delighted congregations for years.

The recitations well learned by heart. Some very long, some in Yorkshire dialect, but reading them was not allowed in this family. Here is one from their programme.

Come have "just one glass" with us, man.
There's surely no harm in that.
One glass won't make you a drunkard.
Just one while we have a chat!
In this way the youth was tempted,
But bravely stood his ground.
There's many a one gone under
And in chains of sin are bound.

Are you one of those my brother?
Who believes in "just one glass".
And think the pub is the right place
A pleasant hour to pass.
Well if you enjoy the laughter and like the fun and life
There's no harm done you say, friend.

Oh! But what about your wife.

She's at home with the children
With plenty of work to do.
I believe you, my friend, but why are you not with her now
The care of the house and children?
Bring much anxious thought and strain,
'Tis yours to comfort and cheer her
When the evening comes again.

One glass won't make you a drunkard.
You may say and believe it's true.
But stay and consider my friend
For the drink may master you,
The man who is now a drunkard.
He said just one glass at the first
Now barrels of drink will never
Quench the demon of his thirst.

For the taste of drink gets stronger,
It weakens the will and brain.
Till nothing can stand before it
All efforts appear in vain,
When the life and health are shattered and home in a desolate state,
And dear little children are suffering, remorse will cry its two late,

And then there are some you know, friend,
Born with the taint in their blood
In them the taste once awakened
Sweeps all away like a flood.

In this we must keep our brother,
Or else we shall be like Cain.

For whatever way we take it,
Drink will go from bad to worse,
And talking will never make it,
A blessing and not a curse.
As Christians and as brothers, let us stand for what is right.
With God as our shield and shelter, press onward and win the fight.

The family were involved in the helping the Turner Family to start the Bridlington Brethren Assembly where they sang at many of the Gospel Tent Campaigns. They had many years fellowship and friendship with the Turner family, who had a market garden at Bridlington and were very much part of the Brethren in Bridlington when the Charter Family moved their beloved friends. The Turners kept in touch and some lovely times of fellowship and teas were had on the various farms.

Shortly after moving to Barmston, an evangelist came to Beeford. The Charter family went to the weeknight meetings; he asked them to sing for him. They obliged with their usual selection of solos, duets, and quartets. The meetings were very successful. A great interest was created, and a good work was being done. The family were happy to be of assistance. After some weeks the family heard the Gospel Tent was coming to Bridlington, they decided to attend. This a decision which cost Vera a great deal of heartache, for the evangelist and work at Beeford received much blessing from the Lord, with lost souls being saved, whilst the tent in Bridlington was not blessed in the same way.

One of the tent campaigns at Bridlington that the Charter Family were singing at came right in the middle of hay time and it was lovely hay weather too. Every night the brothers and sisters downed tools and away they went to sing. Their father was not pleased and their neighbour, Jack Brown from the Old Hall, gave them a rough time of it.

"You'll regret this when it's pouring with rain and we've all our hay gathered in."

The campaign finished and that night it poured with rain. The family only had one field of hay left to gather in. Of course, Jack came over.

"I told you so."

Their father was venting his anger at breakfast time when Vera had the urge to go and see the hay. She got her bike out and went to the field. She thought that hay looked dry and picked some up. It was bone dry. She walked about the field and it was all dry; so, she hastened back home and got all the family into action. The neighbours could not believe their eyes when these loads of dry hay were coming into the village.

". . .if any man serve me, him will *my* Father honour." John 12:26

Chapter 7

CHICKEN BROTH

ON THE MAIN ROAD, THE A165, at the road junction for Barmston, there was a bend notorious for accidents. Cars were becoming more plentiful and going faster; so an ambulance box was put on the side of the road, as at the nearest house, the family was given a key. Vera was first at many accidents, hearing the bang of the accident or sliding of braking wheels while she was going about her daily duties.

One night her sisters were in bed and she was leaning out of the bedroom window when she heard a car approaching the corner. She noticed the beams from the car's lights go around their fields, and then all went quiet.

She yelled to her sisters, "It's crashed!"

Vera hurried down the stairs and lit a stable lantern. Her mother pleaded with her not to go, saying it was someone having her on.

"I've got to go. Someone's injured."

Racing up the road, she could see the car's lights at a strange angle. On arriving she found a man sitting on the side of the road beside a sports car which was on its side; he was badly injured and groaning. Vera unlocked the box and attended to him the best she could and was about to go for help when she saw the lights of another car approaching. She ran up the side of the road, flagging the car down with a lantern. She told them there had been an accident.

The driver jumped out and whispered not to say anything. Then he asked, "Is it a sports car?"

Vera assured him it was and as they walked back up the road, he said he was expecting this and asked Vera if she would go back to his car and keep the young lady from coming to the accident as it was her boyfriend that had crashed. She was his sister and he would not let her travel with her boyfriend because he had been drinking heavily. The young lady was extremely anxious and kept asking what sort of car it was. Vera answered as negatively as possible. Returning the brother told her it was her boyfriend and that the emergency services were sent for. Several days later the family phoned the garage further down the road and asked them to thank Vera for her assistance and to say he was doing fine.

Vera was first to many more accidents. She had no first aid training but read what she could from the literature that was in the ambulance box to keep up with the treatments and remedies.

One of the crashes involved Amy Johnson of aviation fame.

Vera went to a large lorry with three men in it which had overturned, landing on its side. She ran home, took a small ladder, and put it on the bottom of the lorry, and then went up and stood on the top (which was the lorry's side) and was able to open the door and placed a piece of wood across so one of the men could pull himself out—with her aid as she tugged at his clothes. The middleman had a broken arm but managed to climb out. Then Vera went to the garage and phoned for an ambulance.

Her father usually took to his bed in winter, claiming ill health. One day a neighbour arrived with a tureen wrapped in a tea towel.

"I've brought Father chicken broth. I thought it would be a change."

Vera's mother thanked her and as father had a very good appetite collected a spoon from the kitchen and took the container upstairs to him. She had just returned downstairs when a loud wail came from upstairs.

"Mother! Mother! Can you come?"

Vera's mother asked, "What's wrong now?"

Upstairs she went. Coming down a few minutes later carrying the tureen, she was bent double in mirth—this from a lady who seldom even smiled. She stood the tureen on the table and lifted the lid. The poor neighbour had forgotten to take the crop out when she prepared it. All the wheat and grit floated on the top.

Vera was much amused when she had to go to Driffield on business. She told Mrs. Brown, her neighbor, she was going.

She said, "Would you bring me half a dozen jam tarts from Miss Hopes, but don't tell Jack?"

Cycling down the road she met Jack Brown. "I hear you're going to Driffield. Would you bring me half a dozen cream buns from Miss Hopes, but don't tell the missus."

Vera thought it should have been the other way around—the husband having the tarts and the wife the buns, but she carried out her mission competently.

Vera was always very wary of what she read in the papers. Barmston drains blocked and the press arrived at the coastal village, went to Jack Brown's at the Old Hall, and asked if the maid would stand and hold a couple of lambs in the pool of water that had gathered in the field. The maid said she dare not touch the lambs. Ted Hackett, the shepherd, would never let her so she went to the sty and picked up two piglets. In the paper there was an article about the floods at Barmston and a photograph with the caption "Maid Rescuing Piglets from Flood Water".

It was while at Barmston in 1933 that Vera purchased the family's first car—a Humber. A friend, George King, was selling his and Everard liked it a lot. They needed a car, but Father was adamant they were not having one. Vera got all the family together—except her father and mother—, told them to back her up, and bought it for £23. Their father was not happy but everyone else was delighted. The strange thing was Vera was the only one who never learned to drive, although she could take a tractor on the farm if needed but it had to be an emergency.

The family also bought their first tractor for £128, which was new. The money took a lot of finding as eggs were a shilling a dozen and milk four pence a pint.

Taking visitors as well as working outside on the farm was hard for Vera. Her Mother was superb at making bread and cooking dinners, though she often annoyed Vera as she would not put the Yorkshire Puddings in the oven until the visitor's car was approaching which was understandable. Her mother assumed the visitors would want a chance to freshen up before they sat down to their meal. Vera on the other hand would have liked to have had dinner on the table the minute they walked in. For when they had eaten, pots were washed and cleared.

Her mother was never one for cleaning up. Vera had to do her work outside on the farm. The family all had their own jobs and visitors or not turnips were to hoed and hay made; this was when the brothers and sisters would walk up to the beach and Vera was able to catch up with her farm work and bake and clean for visitors if it was needed.

It was while living at Elm Tree Farm that the family saw the only white Blackbird and white Pheasant that they were ever to see.

Moving to Barmston from Driffield on April 6, 1930, at nineteen years of age, it was a new life living in the country. In December of that year Vera had to travel to Driffield on business for her father, who told her not to return until she had seen the businessman himself. She was told by the gentleman's wife that he was away from home and would not return until after five o'clock. Business accomplished Vera caught the bus to Bridlington at 7:45 pm, asking the driver what time the next bus went to Barmston. He said it had already left but offered to take her on his motor bike. She thanked him but declined his offer, saying she had friends in Bridlington.

She got off the bus and decided not to trouble any one since she could soon walk the six miles. When Vera arrived to the last gas lamp, a wall of blackness hit her. Only being in the country for eight months she was used to street lighting. Vera set off once or twice only to return to the last gas lamp, finally knowing she would have to go home. She prayed to her Heavenly Father to go with her trusting in His promise: **"I *will be* with thee" Isaiah 43:2.**

She set off walking as quickly as possible. About two miles from home she met a person on a bicycle. Thinking it was her brother, Everard, coming to meet her she said, "Hello."

Then she realised it wasn't him. About a mile from home a car met her. She heard its brake and turning around, she saw in its headlights a man following her, but the car kept going. Vera started to run and managed to take her torch from her handbag all the while hearing the footsteps gaining on her. At the end of the woods, Vera thought her mother would be looking for her and started to flash her wee torch on and off.

All of a sudden, a loud voice called, "Is that you Vera?"

Her mother had been so worried that her father had come to the corner to meet her.

"Yes!" she yelled. "And be quick there's a man following me!"

She heard her would be attacker go running back up the road. The Lord is truly merciful hearing and answering the faintest cry.

"The Lord *is* nigh unto all them that call upon him, to all that call upon him in truth. He will fulfil the desire of them that fear him: he also will hear their cry, and will save them." Psalm 145:18-19

In the 1930s there was a recession. Farmers were hit hard in the pocket, really struggling for a living. Several, like the Charter Family, had to turn to taking in paying guests. A farmer and his wife further down the road had to turn to this means of income. Vera had occasion to call one day. She was in the kitchen talking to the farmer's wife and her daughter. The farm workers had vacated the kitchen after they had their meal. Their used crockery and cutlery awaiting washing, as the mother and daughter were preparing the meal for the paying guests, the daughter lifted a large spoon off the dirty cutlery, put it in a large pan of custard, gave it a stir took a spoonful out, tasted it, and then put the rest back in the pan.

When she gave it another stir, Vera said, "Hey you can't do that."

"Why? What's wrong?" asked the daughter.

"That's a dirty spoon you have tasted the custard with and put the dregs back in the custard."

"Oh well, what the eye never sees, the heart never grieves about."

So much for hygiene.

Vera and her sisters were very friendly with the Watson family at Ulrome. Annie, Frank, Jack, and Tom, and the sisters walked to the Ulrome Methodist Chapel from Barmston to an anniversary service and, as usual, they went for supper and singing to the Watson's home. It became rather late. The Watson's insisted on seeing them home since it was a two and half mile walk on an unlit road.

Lilian, as always, the independent one and concerned about what her father would say if some young men had seen them home, tried to stop them but to no avail. When they arrived at the main Hull – Bridlington road, Lilian insisted, "We're alright now you can go home."

"No way, definitely not. This is the worst stretch of road."

Lilian, as assertive as ever, insisted that they go home. Seeing she was in that kind of mood; it was no use arguing. The Watsons turned back and headed for their own home.

The sisters made good progress and when they were nearly at the junction to Barmston, a lorry came up behind. When it drew level, it stopped.

"Jump in lasses," a voice from inside said.

"No, thank you," said Lilian in a matron-like voice.

"Come on! There's only three of us."

Alarm bells sounded. The passenger door of the lorry was opened, effectively splitting the girls apart. Lilian and Rosie in front and Vera, behind Rosie, took to her heels and ran as fast as she could.

Lilian waited for Vera.

A voice from inside the lorry yelled, "Jump out, lads, there's a b----- behind!"

Vera, grabbing the edge of the door, slammed it shut with all her might, shouting, "No, there isn't! Run for it, Lil!"

As the lorry went around the traffic island, it put its lights out so they could not read its number. Vera was never known to run but she would have taken a bit of catching that night.

Mrs. Brown came across to Elm Tree Farm. She had a high pitched voice which resounded round the kitchen.

"Can you come across, Vera? Something smells in our kitchen."

Once in the kitchen, Vera said the stink was unbearable. "Oh, Mrs. Brown something must be dead."

"I know, but I've been everywhere and cannot find a thing," replied the distressed lady.

They went around and around, unable to locate the source. Eventually, Vera went across to where the workmen's coats were hung.

"It's over here, Mrs. Brown," she said and began searching the coats. Sure enough, in one of the coat pockets, was a dead rat.

They had a threshing day and one of the lads had put it in another's as a joke. Because of the warm weather, the man to whom it belonged did not put his coat on, but just took it and hung it in the kitchen and after several days things began to hum!

At two o'clock one morning, Vera heard a cow walking up the road. Looking out of the window, she saw the cow go by.

She shouted, "Lilian!"

Quickly dressing, they set off after her. Eventually overtaking her, they brought her back and put her in a field only to be awaken at six o'clock next morning by the publican.

"You eh ma coo I yoor field?"

"Yes," Arthur replied, "It would have been at Hull now but for my daughters getting up at two o'clock and putting it in our field."

Cycling home from Driffield after being to the town on business, it was dark and foggy. In the faint cycle lamp, Vera could see the outline of a ghost in the middle of the road. Loving her Lord dearly, she did not believe in ghosts, but was afraid it may be someone in disguise. It had happened once to her grandfather.

Some way off, she dismounted her bicycle and pondered. The thing was definitely moving. Realising there was no way around, she prayed as her Lord had said.

". . .lo, I am with you always, *even* unto the end of the world." Matthew 28:20

She jumped on her bicycle and pedaled as fast as she could. When she got to it, it was a large white horse that had obviously gotten out and it had its back end towards Vera.

With her grandfather it had been different. It was reported that there was a ghost in his local church yard. Reports were coming in. Even trustworthy and reliable people had seen it.

A friend said to her grandfather, "Thornhill, will you come with me tonight and see if we can see this here ghost?"

"I would love to," was the reply. So getting his dog, Vera's grandfather and friend set off. As soon as they got near the churchyard, this white apparition appeared rattling chains and making weird noises. Her grandfather reached down, let the dog off its lead, and shouted, "Go get him!"

The white sheet went in the air and there was a scurrying then a yell. The dog came back with a piece of trouser in its mouth. There never was any more ghosts in that churchyard.

A man knocked on the door, saying that a boar pig was in the road and the children were leaving for school. He was worried for their safety.

Vera and her mother were at home on their own. Vera opened a shed door, went into the road, and got the pig. Looking at it, she knew it was not one of theirs. She informed the neighbours and police that they had a boar pig, asking if anyone was looking for it.

Three men arrived at the farm with a vehicle and trailer. They came from Ulrome.

Vera took them to the shed.

"Who put it in there?" one of them asked.

"I did," Vera replied.

"He is very vicious," they said. "That is why there's three of us."

Vera and Lilian were awakened one night by the ear splitting squeals of a pig in distress. They threw coats over their nightdresses and pulled on Wellingtons. When they got to the yard, they found one of their pigs had its head stuck fast in the five-barred gate at the entrance to the yard. Where they roamed freely, its head was between two of the spars.

One got behind to push the pig up to the gate while the other manoeuvred the head, twisting and turning it to try to release it. All to no avail. They tried everything to release it all the while accompanied by the ear splitting squeals. Nearly admitting defeat, they were pondering what to do next when Vera noticed the spars were a little wider apart further along the gate. So the sisters stood side by side, one pushing and one turning the head. They gradually moved the pig further up the gate. All of a sudden, the pig gave a mighty tug.

The head was released, and the two sisters were sent flying over backwards onto the ground. This was met with loud peals of laughter. Looking up, they saw at a bedroom window their two brothers happily watching the proceedings.

As already mentioned, Vera's father considered himself an invalid and seldom went outside. There were quite a few pigs ready for sale. Vera contacted Mr. Meadley, who usually bought them and always gave them a good price. Vera was working on the farm when she had need to go to the house. On arriving, there Mr. Meadley sat on his horse in the yard talking to her father.

Seeing Vera approaching, he said to her, "You've sent for me to buy some pigs and your father says you haven't any."

"Well, come and have a look at them, Mr. Meadley. There are eighty for sale." Whoops!

Aunt Meg—her mother's sister—and her family from Nottingham came for holidays on the farm. She had three of a family: Dorothy, Marjorie, and Frank. Aunt Meg hit on the idea of sending her daughters castoffs for the sisters to wear on the farm. An idea that was welcomed with open arms. Regularly the parcels arrived as the daughters had good jobs in the city of Nottingham, but Rosalind and Lilian would dive in and virtually end up with a pile of clothes each. As they were taking them out father would say, "That will fit you, Lilian. That would suit you, Rosie."

Then mother would chime in, "Vera's got nothing."

This went on for some time until Aunt Meg came to stay again. Vera told her what was happening. Since she was quite a bit plumper than the other two, only Marjorie's clothes would fit her.

"Oh, don't worry, Vera, I'll remedy that."

Shortly after, another sack of clothes arrived. Rosie and Lilian dived in again and were sharing them out when Everard said, "Just a minute. There is a label on that one."

Sure enough there was the label that read: Vera. Going through them, one label after another came up: Vera. At last, Vera got her fair share of the clothes.

When Vera was a child, Aunt Meg had come to stay with her husband, Uncle Arthur, had gone with the family to the service on the Sunday evening. Vera had to stay at home to look after Rosie.

She went to the pantry to get supper ready but there was nothing for supper. Being a young child, she had no idea of quantities and being on a farm, there was plenty of milk; so, she made a pint of Blancmange and a pint of custard. She set the table for supper putting on the Blancmange and custard. Her mother and Lilian walked through the door and split their sides laughing.

"Look at that! Look at that! For nine people!"

Aunt Meg said, "Well it's a lot better than what you two have done and I can make it go round." And she did.

It was at the Gospel Hall that Vera befriended three sisters, the Miss Goults: Agnes, Phyllis, and Cassie from Bury St Edmunds. No one had spoken to them when Vera invited them back to the farm for a tea.

That first meal was a memorable occasion for them. There was a dish of tomatoes on the table and Phyllis desperately wanted one. Lilian took one, sprinkled it with sugar, and ate it. William took one and reached for bread and butter and made a sandwich. Everard took one and put salt at the side of his plate and dipped his tomato in the salt and bit into it. Phyllis thought, "How do you eat a tomato in Yorkshire?" Then Vera took one and cut it into sections and sprinkled it with salt.

"Oh lovely," thought Phyllis. "That's how I eat them." So she willingly partook of the fruit.

Poems written and sent to the Family by Phyllis

To the Family at Elm Tree Farm

We've much enjoyed our Holiday upon the Yorkshire Coast,

    And Bridlington has not yet lost its charm.

But do you know the portion which appealed to us the most?

The hours we spent at Elm Tree Farm.

Of course, we came upon you at your very busiest,
    When harvest work was all the go.
And what with fowls and pigs to feed, and cows and all the rest,
    We wonder how you found the time for us you know.

We fear that Mr. Charter may have shirked his work just then,
    In order to devote his time to us.
He pondered and debated what to do and when,
    Till we felt we were creating quite a fuss.

We went with him to fetch the cows, from the farthest field,
    (Our heroism you should all commend)
Then hoping that our fears were fairly well concealed,
    We watched the milking process to the end.

Oh, Mrs. Charter's wonderful; she never seems to rest,
    She flits about the house with lightest tread.
And not content with milking, with much zest,
    "I love a bit of harvesting," she said.

It always gives me pleasure to watch others working hard,
    (And this applies to Everard and Will)
But mischievous though the rabbits are, I must say Everard.
    My sympathies are with those rabbits still.

The girls are quite surprising in their versatility,
    One hundred different jobs they seem to do.
From harvesting to housework, driving carts and making tea.

One even does a bit of cobbling too.

Your music is a great delight to all of you I know,
  For those who listened it has a wondrous charm.
I think of two who wish they were hearing even now,
  Those melodies of Judes at Elm Tree Farm.
         P. Goult. 12 09 1935

We wanted to find an original gift,
  To suit some young friends on the coast.
Oh should it be music or should it be books?
  Which would they appreciate most?
But do they possess it already we said,
  How can we be sure they do not.
We thought and we pondered, then pondered and thought,
  Until in the end we sent —what?
Just hankies to Lilian, Vera, and Rose,
  And diaries to Everard and Will.
With Love and good wishes to each of the five,
  From their Sussex friends Agnes and Phyll.
         P. Goult. Christmas 1935

Chapter 8

FAMILIES FIRST FARM IN THE COUNTRY

VERA WAS TWENTY SIX YEARS OLD IN 1936. Her father, with his quick temper getting the better of him after an argument, cycled up to Burton Agnes Hall and handed in the notice for the tenancy of Elm Tree Farm, effectively leaving the family without a home. Vera found one of the few farms that were coming vacant and that might be suitable.

Vera was always one for what she termed "penciling". This was a piece of paper or card—usually a card out of her Shredded Wheat breakfast cereal box. The Shredded Wheat used to come loose in a box with three biscuits in a row and a piece of white card between the layers this was her favourite for "penciling". A piece of cereal carton cut up would suffice if she had not sufficient cards for the job. No cheap notebooks where available.

Everything was worked out in minute detail, income, outgoing, what was essential to live on: when the first milk cheque would come in, when each cow would calve, when each ewe would lamb, roughly when hens would start laying, petrol for the Lord's Day. This was essential as during the week they could catch a bus, cycle or walk. So as these figures covered a much larger farm than Elm Tree Farm and there was not a lot more working out to be done. Vera actually used a ledger, for the final working out.

The family applied and were successful in getting the tenancy of Malton Cote Farm at Ebberston, near Scarborough. This time Vera made sure the tenancy was in the names of A. T. Charter and Sons, so no one person could give up the tenancy. Malton Cote was at that time owned by Sir Kenhelm Caley, who was extremely helpful and understanding. He was most patient at all times with the family especially as they got adjusted to their new way of life. Malton Cote was a much larger acreage than Elm Tree, being five hundred acres, which was a large step to take.

A problem the family had never encountered before was there were two roofs on the house with a flat piece between. As soon as the snows came, the gulley filled, and when it melted, found its way into the house, Vera had to go up and shovel the snow off before any harm was done.

Malton Cote had four large farmyards, so stocking it and working it was a great challenge to the family. They now had no time to take paying guests, so this income was lost.

Vera often cycled to the Gospel Hall in Roscoe Rooms in Scarborough. The people here were kind to her. Everard could be difficult although he and Vera were quite close, and if everything had not gone his way, he would re-fuse to drive the car. If anything upset him on a Saturday, the car would not be going out on the Sunday. If annoyed on the Sunday, the car would not be going out on the Monday, when the Monday Seamer Cattle Market was held. So if they had sent cattle or sheep to the auction, Vera had to cycle to see them sold—an eight mile journey she could have done without.

Her father seldom went outside but tried to control the business, wanting to keep lambs to stock the many acres while the money from their sale was required to pay the rent. On market day, which was a Monday, the family would get the lambs in for loading and hear the cattle wagon coming up the road. Her father would come out of the house and send the cattle wagon and driver away saying there was no lambs to go. Vera and family would race from the buildings, but it was too late for that day.

After one harvest there was about four hundred pounds worth of corn in hired sacks. Vera took a sample to the market to the corn merchant who usually bought their grain. He said it was slightly damp and would have to deduct a shilling a quarter. Vera returned home and explained the problem to her father. He refused to sell it. A few weeks later Everard went into the granary and found the damp corn had heated and gone moldy. It was thrown away and if that was not bad enough, the hired sacks had burst open and Vera spent weeks mending the sacks to return to the hire firm.

Their father was determined that he would not let any of his family marry. They were there to work for him and him alone. Various steps were taken to put off would be suitors. One was never letting them go out alone. Everard was even supposed to go to the cattle market with Vera, but this did not last for long as Everard was never interested in markets. So Vera had to cycle or catch the bus to see their animals sold.

One of the highlights for the sisters were the meetings at Mr. and Mrs. Ruston's farm, who were neighbours. They enjoyed the speakers and singing the good old hymns. They also attended the camp meetings at the Spenceley's farm in Troutsdale. This is where they first heard Austin Hyde, the well-known teacher, preacher, and broadcaster in Yorkshire dialect.

Malton Cote was the most remote farm the family had ever lived on, being just over a mile from the village of Ebberston. Born in the town of Driffield with street lighting—albeit gas lamps—moving to the Village of Barmston although the land and buildings were a mile away, the house was in the village.

At lambing time Vera stayed up most nights. If Lilian stayed up, Rosie had to stay with her. If Everard stayed up, William stayed with him. That meant that two were away from their work next day catching up on their sleep.

When Vera was on duty one night, some lambs had been born and she was making a quick pen for them and needed some dry bedding. Rushing up to a stack with her stable lamp she began pulling handfuls of straw out when she saw something move in the corner where two stacks met. Looking again she saw a man trying to press himself as tight into the corner as he could. Pretending she had not seen, she went to let the yard dog off its chain.

She pointed in the direction of the man and said, "Get on!"

He sped off. The dog returned when she called him, but they never saw this man again on their farm. Vera was fairly sure she knew who it was as someone local who had a reputation for being light fingered.

Although the family usually worshipped at the Gospel Hall in Scarborough, they kept singing both as the Charter Family and also the sisters would supplement Sunday school anniversaries. If the chapel had not many children to raise a programme, the sisters would sing solos and duets to help them.

When there were visitors at the Gospel Hall at Scarborough the family often asked them up to the farm, as her mother always excelled at cooking dinners and Lilian excelled at bread making and Vera at baking. At a birthday tea many years later for which Vera had baked, it was noted by a guest there was twenty four different dishes on the table. Her mother never agreed with this. She thought, as she put it, "It was vulgar." Mother's idea of tea was a plate of crisp lettuce arranged to make a bed and a piece of cooked salmon laid on it or a plate of lettuce with a large pork pie in the middle, with usually having plenty of milk. When visitors came Mother nearly always had a junket on the table for tea with a bowl of peaches and a plate of thinly sliced homemade bread and butter.

Two sisters were invited to the farm and on being taken for a walk in the fields. Between dinner and tea, they came across a bed of thistles which pricked their legs. One of them looked down and said, "Surely this is holly."

Some airmen visiting the Gospel Hall were invited back to the farm. After dinner the family suggested a walk round the farm. Vera said she would not go with them as there would be a problem as soon as she spoke. The sheep would hear her voice and they would come running and surround them. She did not want them rubbing their greasy wool on their uniforms.

Vera never used a sheepdog but always called the sheep. She was persuaded to go when the group said she need not speak. They were crossing the field when one of them said something funny and Vera laughed.

Baa! Baa! Baa! All the sheep came running, sheep wool rubbing on the guests uniforms.

Vera's voice carried for miles although she never spoke loudly. A farmer told her he had heard her from two miles away calling the sheep. He even told her the names of the sheep. Once Vera went round the sheep as usual to count them and see if they were all right when she noticed some were missing. Going round the field, she found a wall down, leading into a neighbouring farmer's field. She checked but no sheep were in sight. Seeing the farmer, she went across and asked if he had seen her sheep. He assured her he had not. Puzzled by their disappearance she went round other farms. One of them told her the first neighbour she had asked had them fastened in a shed, so she went to the farm and knocked on the door.

"I understand you do have some sheep of ours," Vera said. As soon as she spoke, she heard some sheep bleat in a shed.

"No, I have never seen them" he replied.

So she walked into the farm yard and yelled at the top of her voice. "Baby face!"

"Baa! Baa!" Came from a shed.

She said, "You have made a big mistake. You have got my pet amongst them."

She went across the yard and opened the door and turned round and no farmer was to be seen.

Everard came in one evening tears raining down his cheeks.

"Come quickly, Billy. I'dells murdering his Missus!"

The family raced to the door and over in the direction of the I'dells farm. They found out later it was the first time they had heard a vixen.

Vera was the only one who would take the rent on rent day. Sir Kenhelm Caley asked her to stay for the rent dinner. She thanked him but refused. One year he persuaded her to stay and at that time Malton Cote, being the largest farm on the estate, he sat Vera at the top table with him, of course this did not meet with approval at home. So when Sir Kenhelm came to the farm with a shooting party, Vera's mother said very unkindly to him, "Do you not think my daughter a very cheeky girl?"

He replied, "Mrs. Charter, I find your daughter a very courageous young lady."

After a particular bad year on the farming calendar, Sir Kenhelm went up to the farm to enquire how things were with them. The family were at work when their mother came looking for them—a very unusual occurrence.

"Can you come? Sir Kenhelm has come to the door and your father has got him?"

"Oh no!" The wail went up.

Vera ran for all she was worth. When she got to the door Sir Kenhelm was very angry, something Vera had never seen.

"Miss Charter I must ask you to leave. You are not farming this farm correctly. According to your father you have not sufficient stock on it. You are owing money all over, and you have not got your harvest. What have you got to say?"

Vera replied, "Well the best I can do is show you."

So she took him into the stack yard and showed him all the lovely stacks of corn and hay. Everard was very talented in making hay or corn stacks. She took him to the yards and fields and showed him the stock the cows and sheep. As they went around, she explained what they had achieved and what they hoped to achieve.

He said, "Will the rent will be ready when its due?"

"Yes," Vera replied. "It's nearly all ready now, we are going to have to sell some of the lambs earlier than we would have liked but it will be there on the day."

"Look, don't sell the lambs. Give me what you can, and I will wait until the lambs are ready to go for the rest. Just tell me one thing why does your father know nothing of this?"

"Father is an invalid and hardly ever goes outside the door. He has not a clue what is going on."

Her father thought that if he said they had not got the harvest and had not sufficient stock and this was bad and that was bad he had got such a bad farm it would be less rent, instead he nearly put them out of a home and business.

Market day was here once again, and some sheep were booked to go. The cattle wagon arrived. The sheep were loaded. The lorry driver asked if anyone would be with them. This was unusual as Vera always went to see the stock sold but this particular day, she could not be there. When the money came in the post for the sheep from the auctioneers it was nothing like what the family were expecting. A short time later some more sheep were sold but this time Vera went to see them sold. She found the pens of sheep and stood a little way off until the auctioneer was nearer. He said, "Now we have some fine sheep for Mr . . ."

Vera shouted out, "No, they are ours!"

"Do you claim them Miss Charter?"

"Yes, they are definitely ours. They have our mark on."

"Right then I'll sell them for Miss Charter."

In the next pens were some old thin sheep in really bad condition. Vera always went to the market with her animals ever after.

There was a disagreement of large proportions within the family before Vera married. Vera left home and went to Scarborough and took on a job as housekeeper to an elderly lady. She was a lovely lady, so easy to please. Vera loved working for her and was so happy. The work was so easy after farm work and Vera enjoyed keeping the lovely home clean and the lady company. The wages were good, and she had every afternoon off. Vera had been there seven weeks then a bomb shell fell, in the form of a tear stained letter from her mother.

Vera loved her mother very much, although they were a family that never showed their love, none of the family ever kissed or even put their arms around each other no matter how long they had been or were going to be apart. They never showed any emotion. None of them were ever seen to be crying, although their mother must have shed a few tears for Vera to receive the tear stained letter.

The letter stated that things at home were far from well, chiefly that the work was not getting done. Everard had taken to the sofa as he was prone to do when difficulties arose. He said it was pointless working when there was no money. It had run out in seven weeks. Vera knew this would happen. Money just slipped through her father's fingers; he would order this that and the other. Things that were not even required on the farm with no thought of where the money was coming from to pay for it. At Driffield, when Everard and William were carting coal and goods around the town, they were working and hauling from morning to night yet there was never any money to spare. Their mother had to turn out the drawers for a few coppers to send the younger ones for essentials.

Vera sadly explained to the kindly lady about the situation at home. The lady begged her to stay and told her she would always be welcome there whatever she decided to do. Vera returned home and went into the house. All the family were in the house talking to a friend who was visiting. Her mother slipped into the back kitchen and said, "Have you anything with you? He's come for tea and there isn't a crumb in the house."

Vera said, "Give me some money and I'll bike back to the shop."

"But there isn't any money in the house," said Mother. "That's why I wrote you."

Vera had to cycle down to the shop and spend some of the money she had earned in Scarborough.

Vera immediately started to train Rosie in financial matters in the hopes the situation would never be repeated.

Being war time, food was rationed the cottage. Malton Cote became vacant and Lilian and Rosie decided to go and live there. This on their part was a good move. Anything that was food kept disappearing from the farm pantry and appearing at the cottage. It was soon discovered that all the fat was going was going into a pans of chips for two, so they were soon made to go back to the farmhouse.

Tea was rationed. The family were big tea drinkers; their friends from Bury St Edmunds came to the rescue when they could.

> To Mr. and Mrs. Charter and Family, Malton Cote Farm.
>
> For Yorkshire Folk especially,
>
> It's sad to be denied their TEA.
>
> Denied the "Cup that Cheers" them so,
>
> Which when they're cold creates a glow.
>
> Yet when they're hot, it cools and soothes,
>
> And often tired frowns it smooths.
>
> One would have thought that those who toil,
>
> To gather in the Harvests spoil.
>
> Might justly claim and extra ration,
>
> Seeing they help to feed the nation.
>
> Whether as hired help or not,
>
> Appears to be beside the point.
>
> Such is, however, the decree,
>
> For Malton Cote NO EXTRA TEA.
>
> But though the law unkind may be,
>
> Still you shall have your extra tea.
>
> For what a jot twill be to us,
>
> To feel we can help you thus.
>
> The Tea's our own so don't refuse,
>
> We're free to give it where we choose.
>
> For Yorkshire folk especially,

It's hard to be deprived of tea.

So dears, accept a cup of tea,

From two old friends at B.S.E.

P. Goult. 22 – 10 - 1940

At the cattle market at Seamer, Vera was in the rabbits and poultry shed looking in the various cages when a farmer came to her and asked if she had seen anything of interest. They got into conversation and later as Vera was walking to the bus stop the young man drew up in a car and asked if she wanted a lift.

"No, thank you." she said not really knowing the young man.

"You'll be safe, Miss Charter." a voice from the back of the car said.

"Eddie's alright and he lives near you."

Looking into the car, she saw a dear old friend she knew well from going to Seamer Market, Robert Temple from Sawdon.

"But I don't know him."

"Probably not, but you live above Snainton and he lives above Sawdon and your farms nearly join each other. There's just a farm between. If you come up to Sawdon with us, you can walk across the fields. It isn't far."

As they had different approaches to their farms Vera always went up from either Ebberston or Snainton and Eddie went up to his Farm via Sawdon so they had never met. On this occasion Eddie took Vera to his farm and showed her how to go across two of his fields and one of Mr. I'dells; then she knew where she was and just had two of their own fields to cross.

After this Eddie regularly took Vera home. Of course, he always had Vera's dear friend, Robert Temple, with him whom she found out was Eddie's uncle.

Eddie was a staunch Church of England, although he did take Vera to the Gospel Hall in Scarborough on a Sunday evening for a while after they married.

Before they were married, Vera invited Eddie to the camp meetings at Mr. and Mrs. Spenceley's at Troutsdale, a neighbouring valley. The sisters were quite taken with him, and teased Lilian about him. This was all right as Lilian was their father's favourite and would do as he said. Before things started to get serious, they used to invite him home for supper after the meetings. After one visit Lilian said, "I think Eddie is getting fond of our Vera."

"Then he comes here no more," replied an irate Father.

Vera, who by this time was fond of Eddie, said, "All right but I can go there."

There was a big row, but Vera stood her ground. The hostilities from the family were now a force to be reckoned with. All of them banding together to try to stop the errant one escaping from the family fold. The family liked Eddie well enough and he was from a good family, but they did not want to lose a good worker.

While courting Eddie, Vera would walk over to his farm to see him as the opposition from her family made normal dating impossible. Eddie would look across the fields, see the bull run across the field, and started walking down by the fence. Eddie would know that Vera was on the other side. The poor old bull hated Vera. After they were married, Vera had washed two dresses and hung them on the line to dry. Eddie was taking the bull across the yard when the bull saw the dresses. Vera heard peals of mirth and went to investigate. The bull was charging one, then turning round and charging the other.

Eddie was bent double laughing, "My word, lass, he thought he'd got you that time."

"Get him off, Eddie, he will tear them."

It was wartime and food was short. Eddie's family made their own butter. Eddie had been in the habit of taking some over when he visited, now only Vera and her mother partook of it. Even though butter was rationed and there were shortages, the rest of the family would not touch it. In return, Vera stayed up at night after the others had gone to bed to knit Eddie socks, still doing her farm work during the day.

One day Vera went into the house from the fields unexpectedly and she heard peals of mirth as she opened the door. She went in to find the entire family sat round and her mother stood reading Vera's diary aloud to them. Vera kept it hidden in a drawer but her mother with no shame had searched for it until she found it—and this was the shameful episode poor Vera opened the door upon.

Vera started to go to furniture sales to purchase things for her intended marriage and new home. Everard refused to fetch her purchases home, so Eddie had to go and pick up the things and put them in a shed on the farm.

Eddie collected Vera any used coats or thick garments which she used to clip them for rugs which she prodded when she came in on a night.

"You are not taking those rugs when you get married," was the challenge laid down.

"Well, they are not your clothes or Hessian sacks that they are made of. So they are not yours," was the reply.

"Yes, but you made them in our time," her father said. Vera still had to sneak them out of the house.

The wedding was planned for March 28, 1941. Eddie's mother was a widow and his sister, Grace, lived with her at Sawdon Heights. They were going to live in a cottage they owned in Sawdon Village when Eddie married, and he and Vera were moving into the farm. Eddie's mother inherited much property and land in Sawdon from her grandmother Mrs. Ward.

Vera's family would have nothing to do with the wedding and none of them attended. Everard did relent as the day became nearer and told Vera to buy herself something she wanted, and he would pay. Vera never did as she realised he had no money of his own and would have got into serious trouble if he had asked for any.

Friends and relatives stood by Vera, presents started coming from all over the country. It was war time, but they were digging into their cupboards and drawers. Vera received beautiful gifts and useful ones; things essential to a bride. Her Uncle John and Aunt Doris had a grocers shop on Victoria Road in Driffield and they packed Vera a tea chest of useful items. Bedding, tea towels, oven cloths, dish cloths, dusters, tablecloths, dressing table and sideboard runners, clothes pegs, even a dustpan and brush. Nearly all her life Vera spoke of certain things as being a wedding present from Uncle John and Aunt Doris.

Mrs. Jack Brown from Barmston and Mr. and Mrs. I'dell neighbours gave beautiful crystal bowls.

Mr. Ernie Megson Station Master at Snainton volunteered to give Vera away and Kit Craggs offered his car and driver free for the day and took Vera to Snainton Chapel where she and Eddie were married. Vera arrived at the chapel to find it filled. Word had got round about her family having nothing to do with it so all her friends had decided to take matters into their own hands and get there to support Vera and Eddie. Eddie's mother said if Vera's family were having nothing to do with it neither was she, although Eddie's sister, Annie, who was already married, gave them a beautiful dinner service which Vera used for best all her life. Sister Mary gave them money, but none attended the service, except for Eddie's Uncle Robert Temple and his wife. Vera's many friends from Ebberston Chapel hired a bus to take them to the service.

Chapter 9

MARRIED LIFE

VERA AND EDDIE WENT STRAIGHT into the farm and as soon as she changed, Vera was lambing an ewe, which was experiencing difficulties.

Eddie was never sympathetic to Vera's singing although he liked to hear her sing; he himself played the piano quite well. He did not like her going to the various chapels, which she so loved, and taking part in the anniversaries. It was also the end of the Charter Family as a group; they never sang together again.

Vera had a pet cat, which she adored, but the family would not let her take it with her. This broke her heart and although kind to them never loved a cat again. The cats loved her and if in the field hoeing or cleaning turnips or building a dry stone wall, a row of farm cats would be sitting on a wall near her. Vera was never keen on them in the house. Although when her son, Edward, was small, he had a ginger cat which was allowed in the house. It actually was a problem to keep it outside. Once when he was desperately ill with pneumonia, the cat climbed up the roof and through the bedroom window to get to him. In later years, he adopted a stray or rather it adopted him, and it was allowed into the house, but Vera never loved another cat. Her heart had been broken.

Vera had a lot more jobs in the house now with farm workers living in, but she still loved to get outside when she could. When she saw it was Eddie's job to cut the turnips for the dairy cows, she would slip quietly down the yard, cut the turnips, and fill all the cows cribs. Carrying the huge scuttle under her arm, all winter long she did this task, swinging the cutter handle around and filling the scuttles. One day Eddie came round the corner.

"What are you doing?" he stormed. "Leave that alone. Its Willie Marshall's job."

"But I have cut them all winter for you." she stammered.

"You what?" he demanded.

"I've cut them all winter. I knew it was your job and I wanted to save you." she said.

"But I've been paying Willie Marshall extra for cutting them for me."

"Has it never struck you as funny that Willie's never cut them other winters?" Vera said.

"No, now you come to say he has not."

"That's because I have been cutting them for you." Vera replied.

The first Christmas at Sawdon Heights was Vera's first away from her family. She was now thirty-two years of age and she knew she would find it a bit lonely. But nevertheless, she made her Christmas cake, and iced it, and her Christmas puddings. Vera never made one but three or four, tied them in pieces of old sheet, and hung them from the kitchen ceiling.

She made her stuffing and excitedly got all her bits and pieces for her and Eddie's first Christmas together. The big day arrived and with it a such a dense fog she could not see out of the windows. It was a real "pea souper." The live-in farm workers were on holiday and had gone to their homes. The rest were given the day off, too.

Eddie went to the village with the milk. Vera prepared the dinner the stuffing, bread sauce, roast potatoes, vegetables—the lot—with the greatest of care knowing Eddie had to be careful what he ate, having had stomach problems in early life. Twelve o'clock came and went. One o'clock went by. She thought, well if something had happened, an accident, or anything, someone would have come and told her. There were no telephones. Obviously, she was worried but being hungry sat down and nibbled at her own dinner, which by this time she did not feel like eating.

She ate her pudding. There were no hot plates to keep meals warm. She washed up and cleared all away it now being three o'clock. At four o'clock she started to prepare tea. She put it on a pretty cloth she had kept especially for special occasions, set it with the carefully prepared delicacies, as only Vera could with such love and care. Eddie loved cakes and sweets, and this was to be their first romantic Christmas.

Six o'clock. She was getting really worried. She made herself a cup of tea—all appetite gone. Never in all her life had she been so miserable and at Christmas. At ten o'clock the door opened, Eddie walked in, took his hat and coat off, and hung them up.

"Where have you been?" asked a broken hearted, tearful, lonely Vera.

"What me? I have been at my mother's. I knew she would be lonely today. It is her first Christmas without me."

Vera falteringly answered, "But she has Grace living with her and Annie and her family just down the street and I had no one. I have been on this isolated farm all on my own, in this dense fog. I couldn't see a thing."

"Oh, I never thought." replied Eddie.

It could have turned anyone against Christmas forever, but when Vera had her own children, she made Christmas very special with what she could afford. She always loved Christmas and all that goes with the celebrations.

Eddie was never good at showing affection. Born at Bedale Grange, Wykeham, on the August 8, 1906. Eddie was a private person. As a young man he had purchased four large wooden huts on wheels. He was a hoarder, something that came from his mother's side. Her Uncle Jacksie Ward was renowned in the Sawdon area for hoarding anything and everything.

There was only one thing that Jacksie loved more than his hoarding and that was Vera. When Eddie and Vera were first married, occasionally Vera would ride down to the village with Eddie, especially if they were combining taking the milk down with a shopping trip. Eddie would slip into his mother's to see if she wanted anything and Jacksie would slip out to the car to talk to Vera. He loved to speak of the Lord and spiritual things and of course Vera also loved to speak of her Lord and Saviour. He never shaved and had long hair. He said he never had it cut because the Lord Jesus had long hair.

The war was still on. One day after shopping, Eddie had gone into his mother's with her groceries. Jacksie came to the car. Vera mentioned that they had been all over Scarborough looking for an enamel washing-up bowl.

When Eddie came out of his mother's, Jacksie said, "Eddie, when you come down with the milk in morning, there will be some apples just inside the gate. Take them. They will be for Vera."

Eddie, unthinking picked up the apples, and took them home. Vera could not believe her eyes. The apples were packed in a lovely enamel bowl—just what Vera was wanting to wash her pots in. When Vera thanked him, he said "Vera, you can have anything I have."

After that, he used to ask Vera if she was wanting anything. She was all right as many apples, plums, and pears were always placed in receptacles that might come in useful and set at the back of the gate. A few years later when Vera and family were living at Woodhouse Hackness, Eddie heard from a neighbour that Uncle Jacksie had passed away.

He said to Vera, "I must go and see my mother."

Sawdon was only a few miles distant through the forestry. He arrived to an unusual scene; he was surprised there was no one in at his mother's. He went up to Jacksie's; hearing voices he went in and looked around. He saw all his family were there, even his brother and his wife from Middlesbrough.

Eddie was the only one his mother had not contacted. This hurt Eddie as he and Vera were fond of Jacksie, but he said nothing. All the rooms in the house and the sheds outside were full a lifetime's hoarding. They had to be sorted. The family had to carefully and painstakingly go through boxes within boxes containing everything including, nails, stubby bits of pencils, odd bits of chalk, safety pins, odd beads, and broken jewelry. Larger boxes would contain rusty gate fasteners, door hinges, nuts, bolts, screws all in various stages of disintegration, lots either rusted or rotted through; yet all had to be gone through meticulously as odd pieces of money was hidden in various ways—coins in tins of buttons and bank notes hidden in pages of books. To Eddie it must have felt like home as all his huts and sheds were filled with all manner of items in old metal hat boxes. Metal army ammunition boxes were full and neatly stacked in their own places, and Eddie knew where each was and what was inside them.

A lady called one day and said she was ordering some red roses. Going on at length with a list of choice blooms, "I have ordered Ena Harkness and Peace."

"No, no" cut in Eddie. "Peace is not red."

With which Vera agreed. The lady became irate, so they said no more. Eddie rose from his seat and quietly went outside returning a few minutes later with a pile of nursery catalogues, all opened at the delicate pale creamy Peace. He showed them to a very embarrassed lady she left in a hurry.

As a good cricketer, he played for Wykeham. Vera kept a cutting from a paper: *E. Stonehouse 30 Not Out*. There was a debate amongst the workman. It rose into an argument concerning a county player. Eddie kept quiet in the background; the next day, armed with cricket books from his sheds, he went to correct the errant ones. The daily papers Eddie received—items of varied interest from local news to the land speed record—were all cut out, insurance adverts, car prices, everything had its own tin.

All his life if he could not be found, he would be in one of his huts.

Having health problems was always a handicap to Eddie. He, as a young man, was one evening in great pain and dizziness; he was unable to stand and was sent to bed. The doctors never got to the bottom of the problem and he was diagnosed as having a dropped stomach. His mother and wife could cope with this but no one else could. His mother would give him bland foods, eggs in milk, cake, and light foods. When he married Vera, she would give him eggs, cooked lightly and in breadcrumbs, milk puddings, and light sponges—diets for invalids were not as advanced then. It caused Vera concern all his life as she was sure he was not receiving sufficient nourishment. The greatest cause of worry for her were well meaning friends, neighbours, and relatives were visiting, knowing full well Eddie's problems, would sit him down to a roast beef dinner saying, "This will do you good. You don't get anything like this at home."

Going threshing corn at a neighbours, they would give him stew and suet dumplings. A well-meaning workmate would see cake and light food in Eddie's lunch box and give him a ham sandwich. Eddie was well brought up and always had impeccable manners. The last thing he would do would be to refuse to eat it but would arrive home in agony; and first his mother, then when he married Vera, would have to see him in pain.

Eddie's mother and Grace came up for tea. No special occasion, but Grace and Vera were quite fond of each other. In the window was a jardinière that Eddie's mother had not taken when she left the farm. Vera put her beautiful double white geranium in it; Vera loved it. The next day Eddie came back from taking the milk and said, "Oh, Mother wants that jardinière. It's hers. She did not mean to leave it."

He picked it up and went walking to the door with it.

"Just a minute, Eddie. She can have the jardinière, but the geraniums are mine!" Vera exclaimed.

"Oh, she wants the plant as well." Eddie replied and went off with it.

After the war was over rationing continued for some years. Eddie had taken Vera to see her family in the car after she had been shopping. When they left, her mother went to open the gate. The grocer had told Vera a few Blue Riband biscuits had come in and would she like some. Delighted, she accepted the kind offer. As her mother was opening the gate, Vera said, "I will give Mam the Blue Ribands. She may never live to see any biscuits back on the market."

So, she gave her the pack of six. "There, Mam, there is six one for each of you."

"Oh, a Blue Ribands. I never thought I'd see another."

Sometime later Everard went over to see Vera about something. Vera said, "Did you enjoy your Blue Riband biscuit?"

"What biscuit?"

"The ones I gave to Mam for you last time we were over."

"I have never seen a biscuit since the war started," he replied.

The next time Vera saw Lilian she asked, "What happened to those biscuits? Everard said he never had one."

"Yes, whatever did you say anything to him for? There was a row! Rosie and I saved them to have with our cups of tea."

When the family moved to Malton Cote, Vera was dreading going to the local cattle market at Seamer. She had attended Driffield cattle market since being a child and not only knew the auctioneers and market staff, but also most of the local farmers and dealers.

Women did not go to the markets then and when eventually she had to go with some sheep, she got the surprise of her life. The same dealers and a lot of the farmers who went to Driffield Market also went to Seamer. She couldn't believe it as she walked down pens of sheep, first one farmer then another.

"Hello, Miss Charter, where have you been? We've missed you."

The market was run by Boulton and Cooper and just after Vera was married, she was in the market. Someone had put some hand tools in hammers, drills, screw drivers, and such for sale. Vera bought a tool and the auctioneer, Stan Currie, knocked it down to Miss Charter. There was laughter all around and a comment, "No, no, Stan, where have you been? Vera's married."

"Oh, who's the lucky man?"

"Eddie."

"What? Eddie Stonehouse?"

"Yes."

"Oh, come here," said Stan and Vera and Eddie were ushered forward. Stan stepped down from his rostrum and congratulated them shaking their hands. Vera had never felt so embarrassed but at the same time happy for although there were sad times when parting with a dear old cow or pet sheep, Vera loved Seamer Cattle Market dearly. She not only met her husband there, but all auctioneers, staff, dealers, and farmers treated her with the greatest respect. Mr. Witty, the cashier in the office, was a dear man and Stan Currie and Norman Willis auctioneers were great personalities; they were the main auctioneers during the 1940-1950s.

Eddie's father died the year before Eddie and Vera met. One day Eddie came in with a sheaf of papers.

"I thought you might like to see these. It's the winding up of my dad's estate, if you'd like a look."

Eddie's father had farmed Bedale Grange on Lord Downes Wykeham Estate as well as Sawdon Heights which he owned.

Vera was looking through the papers and she discovered that Sawdon Heights had been willed to Eddie, his brothers, and sisters, but not Eddie's mother to whom they were paying the rent. So, Vera said they should not be paying as much rent, only four-fifths since Eddie was part owner with his brother and three sisters. The next morning when Eddie went with the milk, he told his mother. The day after he did not return from the milk run until late in the day.

Vera said, "Well, where have you been?"

"Oh, I've been comforting my mother. She hired a taxi yesterday to go to see the solicitor and he agrees. You are right. She does not own it. She is very upset."

Thinking she was upset because her son had been paying too much rent, Vera said, "So are we paying less rent then?"

"No! And she says we still have to pay it to her, not to my brother and sisters".

So coupled with the fact Vera was expecting her first child—which she lost when she had been cutting turnips and taken a full scuttle through a gate that was not properly on its hinges; when it fell it knocked her down and the scuttle and turnips landed on top of her—it made Vera very unsettled as Eddie's brother and sisters were always kind to Vera.

As before mentioned, neither Vera nor Eddie's family could show affection. Eddie was knocked out and badly injured when he was trying to start a tractor. He was turning the handle and the tractor backfired and struck him on the head. He had to be taken to the doctor at Snainton. As they came back up Sawdon Village, Vera asked the driver to stop at Eddie's mothers so she could tell her what had happened. And so she could see Eddie. She would not even come to the door to see him in the car, "Oh I'll come up and see him at the farm when he's better." she said.

The rent argument was the end of Sawdon Heights for Vera, but when Eddie's sister, Mary, heard of the reason for them leaving was about the rent, she very generously said they need not pay her share of the rent as she was all right financially; but Eddie's mother, hearing of this, still insisted the full rent was paid and although legally it was wrong, Eddie idolized his mother and insisted she got the rent; although she had the rents from her other properties.

Eddie called in Cundalls and they had a farm sale. Vera had several baking days and set a lovely spread in the front room for the auctioneers. In the kitchen she had plenty of food and copious amounts of tea for friends. Vera's sister, Lilian, had come over for the sale and was helping to serve teas in the kitchen. Vera was needed at the auction for a while. When she returned to the house, Lilian had seated her own nearest neighbours from Malton Cote at the table with neatly pressed white cloth and highly polished silver the best china in the beautifully clean room set for the auctioneers. The delicately cut sandwiches were being wolfed down by hungry farmers in their mud caked wellingtons. Vera was heartbroken.

Eddie said his father used to speak of the time the threshing machine went to Sawdon Heights from Brompton. Straight up the fields there was so much frozen snow, they could not find the road or see the hedges. So severe did the winters used to be, Vera's own grandfather, who came from Nottingham, once drove a wagon and four horses over the river Trent.

Shortly after, Vera had left Malton Cote, which was part of the Ebberston Estate. It was sold on Friday June 27 1941, with Ebberston Hall and several farms and cottages. Northern Dairies purchased Malton Cote. Vera's family stayed on for a while.

Chapter 10

A FAMILY OF HER OWN

ON LEAVING SAWDON HEIGHTS, Vera insisted the money from the sale be invested. There was no suitable property available that Vera could find; she was expecting a baby, so was limited in the work she could do. Eddie had now been injured by a bull. Northern Dairies were leasing a cottage. Vera and Eddie applied for it and got it. Vera's mother and Lilian were pleased but the rest of the family not too suited, yet even they would rather Vera be in it as someone they did not know.

During the first harvest the family asked Eddie if he would give them a hand to lead the corn. Lilian, always a prude, was loading the rulleys; she was desperate for the toilet but dare not say she wanted to go while Eddie was there. However, all was not lost. Eddie had to go home to the cottage for something, so she waited until the load was on, then darted off to a small quarry they called the "pit" in the corner of the field; alas, she had left too late for she was sitting there when Eddie returned. He was a very good runner and was running back; he jumped over the wall into the pit. He pretended he didn't see anything and just kept running. The next morning when Eddie had left, a timid figure arrived at Vera's door.

"Did Eddie see me yesterday?"

Vera teased her for a while pretending she did not know what she was talking about, then she said, "Oh, in the pit? Oh yes, of course, he saw you."

"He didn't! What did he say?"

"He was running so fast he just noticed you were sitting there."

But it cured her from taking too things too far and never minded leaving the rulley again.

Eddie helped Vera's family for eleven weeks and no pay was forth coming, so Vera kept saying to Lilian, "When are you going to pay Eddie? We can't live on nothing?"

"Oh, you will have to see Rosie."

Eventually she saw Rosie. "When are you going to pay Eddie?"

"We aren't. He never came while eleven o clock."

"Yes. you could not start leading until eleven, until the dew went off, but he stayed while eleven on a night."

Eddie never received a penny from them. Vera and Eddie had some money from the farm, but Vera would never allow that to be touched. She always said both Eddie and she, being farmers, they could have some children who wanted to farm. It would be in their blood which is what did happen. The problem was that Eddie no longer wanted to farm and would not let the money be used for such.

Vera's mother and Lilian were very good at popping in to see Vera when she had her baby son, Edward, in November 1943. Vera had been baking for weeks cakes, biscuits, and buns that would keep in tins and had a good supply of tinned food.

Vera was confined for some time. She had received internal injuries when as a child she fell and actually sat in a bowl of boiling curd that her mother had set on the floor to cool. She had a very difficult birth and was badly injured because her son was a very large baby.

One day her mother said, "What have I to do about food?"

"Oh there's plenty in the biscuit tins in the pantry, Mam."

"There isn't anything."

"But I baked loads."

"Well there isn't anything left."

"Where's it all gone?"

"I've been making the nurse a cup of tea and she loves your baking; and Lilian's been coming over and we've been having something to eat with her."

Poor Vera had to find some strength from somewhere as her family's help ran out when the food ran out.

Vera loved flowers, especially small delicate ones. She loved wildflowers and had a good knowledge of them and their habitat although nothing ever came to her as powerfully as her love for scented violets. She would be cycling with her children and suddenly shout, "Wait a minute!"

She would get off her cycle and walk back a few steps and, bending down, search under the hedge and come out with a few delightful violets. They were better than gold to Vera. She knew all the banks around Scarborough where they grew and always tried to gather a few for her mother. When her mother was a child, she had picked a bunch of scented violets. A horse and carriage passed her. Stopping, a gentleman stepped down pressing a coin into her hand asked her if he could buy them for the lady accompanying him.

"Oh, yes, and if you have time to wait, I can pick you some more."

Vera had green fingers and could get almost anything to grow from cuttings.

One particular day she was busy in the garden when her mother came up the garden path with some relatives, "I am just going to show your cousins your lovely house."

"No, Mother, you can't."

"Yes. I want them to see how lovely you keep it."

"No, Mother, you are not." Vera loved her mother dearly but flatly refused.

Later when the relatives had gone, her mother came over. "I so wanted them to see your lovely clean home."

"Mother, you gave me nothing when I got married. All my furniture and linen came from sale rooms and Auntie's. It's all second hand." They would all set off with brand new furniture and linen. You're not making a laughing-stock out of me."

It did not take Vera long to realise she was too near her old home for Comfort. Lilian or her mother would come across.

"Have you a spice loaf or anything? We have company come and not a crumb in the house."

One day Lilian came over, "Can you lend us some blankets? We have to put someone up for the night?"

Weeks went by and the blankets were not returned. Vera kept asking and asking but no sign of any blankets. Vera went across to the farm determined to get her blankets, knowing they would not be looked after and dreading them getting dirty or even moths in them.

"Mother, I've come for my blankets."

"I can't let you have them. You see, Lilian has them on her bed and she can't do without them."

At the chapel, the family met Ernie Bradley from Ebberston—a fine gentleman even in old age. He was as straight as could be, not only in bearing but in business too. His wife was a quiet lady but very kind and considerate. Ernie had quite a bit of land and some large orchards. He was very good to the family and Vera could go down and pick as many windblown apples as she liked. She used to bike down and fill a sack, put it on the handlebars of her bike, and pedal away up Ebberston Dale home. When she wanted any good apples to keep, she just had to say so and Ernie would sell her some.

He knew his trees very well and could tell anyone if that was a crisp apple, or if that was sharp to the taste or very sweet. He even had one which amused him because it tasted like a banana; he knew all the varieties and their names. These apples were a boon to Vera, not only at Malton Cote but for a good many years after. Wherever she moved to, she made lots of blackberry and apple jam. She washed apples, cored them, filled the middle with sugar, and put them on the bottom shelf of the oven when baking. Then she had them for tea.

Chapter 11

TWO SHORT STAYS

EDDIE AND VERA HEARD OF a small holding on Lord Derwent's Hackness Estate. They applied for it and were successful. It was called Woodhouse. They moved there in 1945. Vera was expecting, and it was a heavy task packing up and flitting. Eddie went down with the furniture. Vera had a lovely polished table and sideboard which she particularly liked. When she arrived at Woodhouse, there was no table or sideboard.

She asked Eddie what had happened to them, and he replied, "The farmer that was leaving said they would not go through the door, so I gave them to him."

"Why?" Vera said "Of course they would go through the door. It's same size as the one they came out of. He just said that because he wanted them."

"I never thought," he replied.

Poor Vera's heart was broken many times; she had worked so hard to prepare a nice pleasant little home only to be crushed so often.

Woodhouse was a lonely place on a wooded hillside. There was no road to it suitable for a car. There was only a footbridge over the river; although Vera had good neighbours at the next farm, Mount Misery—Mr. and Mrs. Nesfield—their family all were grown up and either married or working. Here began a friendship that was to last a lifetime. The children were very fond of Mr. Nesfield and called him 'Grandad'. The only grandad they knew was not close to them, although in later years, he was very fond of Edward and slipped him many a useful tool when the family were not looking—probably guilt for the way he had treated Vera. He even started to give the family half a crown on their birthdays until Vera was visiting with the family around Edward's birthday. When her father slipped Edward half a crown, Vera said "Hey where's mine?"

"Where's your what?" said Rosie, who was apparently standing behind her.

"The half-crown for my birthday."

None of the family ever saw another half-crown from their grandfather. Mr. Nesfield would walk on to see if the family were all right if he hadn't seen them for a while and have a 'cuppa'. Even though he was busy, he had to have everything ready when his wife took farm produce to Scarborough Market every week.

Not many folk had cars and the men folk would take their wives to the farm road end to meet the bus, in horse and cart or tractor if they had one. Fred Nesfield, the son, was very helpful and would give Eddie a hand since Vera now had two young children: a baby girl and a toddler son. One evening Fred gave Eddie a hand, and Eddie gave him a ten shilling note, which was quite a new thing to Fred. Working at home, farmers sons and daughters at home were very fortunate if they received any payment since there was not much money around. Farm wages were only a pound or two a week. It was the usual saying, "You'll get the farm when I've gone."

But a bit of spending money would have been very nice, especially when like Vera you eventually got thrown out with nothing in the end. However, Mr. Nesfield was tickled pink with Fred. He went home and they were sat at supper and out came the ten shilling note. He started playing with it, opening it out, and smoothing it flat. His mother looked up.

"Fred, where have you got that?"

With a wry smile, he replied, "Never you mind."

"I do mind. Where did you get it?"

"Never you mind, Mother. It's mine." Then folding it up and putting it his top pocket said, "See this, Mam? In here it's going and in here it stays." Mr. Nesfield was amused as he had a good idea where it had come from.

Eddie had a younger sister, Grace, who was very shy and not strong in health. The doctor said she needed a change. The only place she would go was to Vera's, so Eddie's mother and Grace came for a holiday. How pleased Vera was. It was a time she always remembered with affection.

Eddie was amazed at Vera's knack of making something out of nothing. He would open the door, and the fire would be low.

"Can you rustle up a bit of supper? 'So and so' is here; he is going to help me with a job."

"Oh no, Eddie, we are shopping tomorrow. I haven't a crumb."

Job finished they would go in to a lovely smell of cooking and a roaring fire. Vera had opened a tin of salmon, cooked some of her potatoes from the garden, and made fish cakes. Vera always had plenty of tinned food in her pantry. It was the only thing that kept before fridges and freezers. There would be a bowl of peaches—again out of a tin—and a corn flour pudding like a Blancmange, but warm and a jug of cream. They had a house cow and a dish of homemade biscuits. Eddie often said there was some near squeaks, but she never failed him.

It was dark and Eddie was away. Vera was ironing in the house with her little boy playing on the floor and baby in the cot. There came a tap at the window. Looking up she saw a face looking in at the window. She pretended not to see but the tap came again and looking again she saw it was a soldier.

"What do you want?" she yelled.

"Can I come in a bit?"

"No. you cannot away with you!" Vera shouted looking down at her little family and prayed for the Lord to help and protect her. Calmly she went to the back door picked up the yard brush, crept round the house, and began to rain blows down upon the offending unsuspecting soldier.

"No, no. It's only me, lass. I found this hat coming home I was only having a bit of fun."

But to the isolated young mum it was no fun. She burst into tears and she never ever got over it. The husband, like her father, tried to see what she was made of and both nearly paid dearly for it.

Staintondale

Vera and Eddie moved to Moorside Farm Staintondale but were not there long. Their neighbours were Billy and Dot Nesfield and their three sons, Brian, Harold, and Arthur. Billy was son of Mr. and Mrs. Nesfield, their former neighbours at Woodhouse. They were good neighbours and were quite near which was nice for Vera.

Vera had reason to pop round to Dot's. She took her baby in her arms and was not long, but on returning could hear Eddie playing loudly on the piano. He was a nice pianist normally; when she went inside, she found a heavy coat was over Edward's cot. Throwing it away and checking to see if the little boy was all right, she said, "Eddie what are you doing?"

"He was crying and wouldn't stop, and I couldn't bear it any longer." he replied. Vera never left the children alone with Eddie again.

Vera and family were at Staintondale in the famous 1947 winter of snow, deep snow. Farm sales were put off and put off again. Some as many as three times, but farmers were desperate for in those years farms changed hands on April 6th. After a particular heavy night's snow, Vera and family were well and truly blocked in. Things had been barely passable for some time. They got the animals fed, and Eddie milked the cows; but the family could go nowhere.

Vera started to worry because one of their milk customers at Gowland Lane had a very young family. The children needed milk. So in the blizzard, she took her baby to Mrs. Nesfield, wrapped Edward up warmly, put him on a sled with the milk, and set off; when she arrived at the house the lady was so relieved and very grateful. She sent Vera's children lovely gifts at Christmas.

Vera and Eddie had a heavy or cart horse for farm work. It hit its head on the stable door causing a wound. The veterinarian came to see it; he gave them some ointment, saying it was all right to work with the horse.

Eddie was working with the horse when, who should come into the yard, but the agent for the Duchy of Lancaster who owned the farm. He got out of his car marched up to Eddie and said he should not be using the horse as it had poll evil, a notifiable disease. Eddie said it was not poll evil. He was with her when she struck her head on the stable door. He said the vet had seen her and said she was quite capable of doing her work, he also said, "I have had enough of your interfering. You can have your farm." Then he had to go into the house and tell Vera she was homeless since he'd given notice to quit.

Vera loved the Northern lights and before she left Staintondale there was a magnificent display. She hurried across to Mrs. Nesfield's saying, "Come quick, the Northern Lights are spectacular!"

"Oh no we never look at anything like that."

Vera replied, "If you lived up north you would have nothing else. It is their only light."

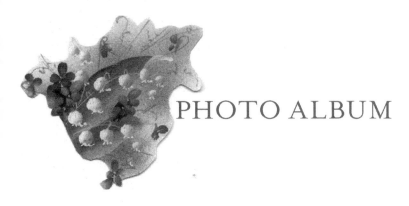

PHOTO ALBUM

A Teenage Vera

Back Row: Lilian, Everard, Two Friends, William, Friend
Front: Rosie, Vera

Vera at Elm Tree Farm,
Barmston

Eddie

Vera at Barmston

William, Everard, and Lilian at Driffield

Left to Right: Rosie, Lilian, Vera, William, Lily, Everard, and Arthur

Vera at Elm Tree Farm

Malton Cote Farm

Father, William, Rosie, Lily, Lilian, and Vera at Barmston

Vera's Mother and Father at Lowdales Farm

Vera and Eddie on their Wedding Day

Vera, Edward, and Sylvia

Vera and Son Edward, born 1943

Vera and Family at Grace's (Eddie's Sister) Wedding

Edward, Albert, Vera, Sylvia, and Marjorie

Vera Gardening at 82 Years of Age

Vera at 93 Years of Age

Vera (center) celebrating her 100th birthday. Author Sylvia Lindsay front-right.

Chapter 12

HAPPY DAYS

WHEN LEAVING MOORSIDE, STAINTONDALE to move to Lowdales, Eddie took several consignments of goods in the car. The thing that amused him most was that his daughter, two-years-old, used to go with him. The house had bare floorboards; so she would race upstairs and run backwards and forwards through the bedrooms, delighted with the echo of her feet on the bare wood.

Eddie heard of Lowdales Farm and cottage on Lord Derwents Hackness Estate, which were becoming vacant. The farm was too much for Eddie as he was not well and it was over two hundred acres; so he told Vera's family, who were not coping at Malton Cote and looking for a smaller place, and took them to see it.

"Never," they said. "It just wants a lid on, and it would be a box."

"Well," Eddie said. "You have to be out of Malton Cote and you have nowhere to go and anywhere is better than nothing."

They did eventually take it and Vera and Eddie went into the cottage, which Vera's family were furious about. They thought they should have had the cottage with the farm. The ones who voiced their disapproval when first seeing Lowdales actually stayed there for forty years.

Vera and Eddie were walking some sheep through the forestry to Hackness for Vera's family; it was very quiet with no traffic when all of a sudden ahead of them a car was approaching. It stopped and out got a man with a yapping terrier, which headed straight for the sheep. Eddie said, "It's the Duchy of Lancaster Agent."

Eddie yelled, "Get that dog in!"

The sheep were terrified and in danger of heading into the woods. The man made no attempt to call in the dog. So Eddie, who was the calmest man on earth unless someone was taking advantage of him, fled through the flock to the front and picked up a stone to throw at the dog.

Then the agent found his voice. "Don't you touch my dog!"

"You call your dog in or you won't have a dog!" Eddie yelled.

Vera, watching from the back of the flock of sheep, saw Eddie taking his coat off and both arms go into the air. She ran to them through the sheep, leaving them to take care of themselves.

"No, Eddie, he's not worth it!"

He got the dog and drove off leaving Vera and Eddie to gather up the sheep.

Vera, although her family disapproved of her being there, made a happy little home at Lowdales. She had a very large garden and it was a pretty little cottage.

Not having the best of health and having two small children, Vera repeatedly told her children of her Lord and Saviour, how much He loved them. She explained how He had died for their sins; she led them both to put their trust in Him. She later told them she thought she may have to leave them without a mother but did not want to leave them without a Saviour.

Edward and Sylvia were taught by Vera to read and write, count, do simple sums, and tell the time before they went to school. Before they were seven, she had taught them to play simple hymn tunes on the piano. After she had taught them the notes and easy tunes, she listened to them once a week and if they could play a hymn with no sharps or flats and made no mistakes, they got a penny. If it had sharps and flats and there was no mistake, they got sixpence. Vera soon realized although practicing just as hard as her brother, Sylvia was never going to be able to play anything without a mistake and worried she would grow disheartened. When she gave Edward his money for his perfect playing, she would give Sylvia a few pence for "trying" and it was Sylvia who ended up playing at many churches but seldom without a mistake.

Edward was not able to commence school when he should because of pneumonia. When he did start his teacher came to Vera as she was cutting out some pictures saying, "I am going to start teaching Edward to read."

Vera replied "Have you tried Edward with his reading? Well you ought," said Vera. The teacher was amazed when Edward could read as good as her.

They had moved to Brompton School when Edward passed his eleven plus, to go to the Scarborough Boys High School as it was known back then. Being told the Headmistress at Hackness replied, "That's his mother pushing him." She must not have had much confidence in her own teaching.

At Lowdales Cottage there were beds of lovely lilies-of-the-valley, pear trees grew up the cottage walls—which were a picture when they blossomed and provided delicious fruit—, and columbines with their gently nodding granny night cap heads. Vera, for every columbine she had, had Lupin the same colour. Vera had rows of delicious raspberries and beds of luscious strawberries. She grew rows of potatoes and vegetables. The paddocks kept the family cow and provided her with hay most of which, at hay time, Vera turned by hand.

Dick Atkinson from Troutsdale used to cut the hay. The small paddocks were level—much of Dick's work was not. When travelling on the road if you saw there was a particularly steep field being ploughed out you could be sure it was Dick on the tractor; he was fearless, yet such a kind considerate gentleman loved by all who knew him.

The water was piped to the door though there was no electricity in the countryside much in the late 1940s. There were four paddocks and, as it was surrounded on the hillsides with trees, Eddie made a large hen run to try to keep the hens from the foxes. With much success it was more the hens, mostly dear old Sussex and Rhode Island Reds, who would find a way out than the fox would find a way in.

It was lovely to see them leisurely walking around scratching for seeds, insects, and grit, especially when Vera had sat a clutch of eggs. The little chickens were allowed in the yard with their mother and had their own coops. A gentle stream murmured close by which was never cause for concern; indeed, it had its uses as it was not deep and when Rosie or Father had been difficult and unreasonable with Vera, the first she could escape unnoticed, Lilian would walk up the river to see if Vera was all right.

There was an abundant orchard in which stood a pear tree. Stately, she stood high on the bank above the other trees always laden with fruit which alas were never eaten and caused great disappointment to any who would try to sink their teeth into the abundant fruit. They were always rock solid however long they were kept.

Eddie built some sheds and a pig was reared. She was a dear pet to Vera's children but very sadly had to provide the household with bacon. Edgar Redman, the Cloughton Blacksmith, was called to come and do the evil deed.

The first time he came Eddie said to Vera, "You stay indoors and don't give Edgar a cup of tea."

"Why ever not?" asked Vera, who kept an open house—a kettle boiling at the ready and a good supply of home baking.

"Well I'm afraid he uses a lot of rather choice words which you would rather not hear. He is a grand chap but it's the language he uses."

"Oh bring him in when he's finished; he's not going without a cuppa." Vera replied.

So in he came, enjoyed his supper, and never spoke a wrong word.

"Well," Eddie said. "I just can't believe it. No one will ever believe that."

While here, Vera was able to keep some poultry to dress for sale. She also had eggs to sell. Shopping day was once a fortnight on a Saturday. Friday would see Vera plucking and drawing these unfortunate fowls for customers.

Her customers were all private. She did not have to take them to the market. Vera made her own butter which she also sold. It was beautiful butter as she never left the cream too long before she made it, so it never tasted rancid like so much farm butter did.

No matter how tired she was in the evening, however hard she had worked that day, it was a case of: "Remind me kids I must make that butter tonight."

She had the glass "blow" butter churn and often as he became older Edward would help her churn it. She had a metal separator that separated the cream from the skimmed milk. These were a pain to wash as they had so many awkward parts but had to be done often. Although a boiling kettle of water was sent through after use, the milk could still collect in nooks and crannies and once again this would cause the cream to go off and the butter to taste rancid.

Eddie asked Mr. Butt, the Hackness Estate manager, if he could have permission to take the car up to the house and put a garage up. This was granted, but Vera's family would not allow him to take the car past the farm. He could have persisted as he had the Estate's permission and they owned the farm, but Eddie and Vera were all for a quiet life though this meant on a Saturday Vera had to walk to Hackness where the car was garaged—nearly two miles with two little children and baskets of butter, chickens, and eggs; yet her family were regularly at Vera's door asking for baking if they had company come unexpected.

Vera was the largest of the three sisters in both ways—taller and plumper. Shopping in Scarborough, she saw a sale and bought three pretty dresses at ten shillings each. Knowing what colours her sisters liked, she called in at the farm as she went by to leave them. Lilian was thrilled with hers, but Rosie wanted to see what Vera had got for herself. Vera said it was no good as it was much larger and longer. Eventually she showed her it and Rosie said if she could not have that one, she was not having any. Vera said, "The one I got for you won't fit me, and mine is too big for you."

Rosie was adamant and would not let Lilian have hers either, so Vera was landed with three dresses—two which would not fit her. So that was goodbye to her hard earned egg and butter money that week.

Something that caused Vera great distress when Edward was nearly four. Eddie and Vera took the children to Flamborough to see the lighthouse. While looking around the outside of the lighthouse, the foghorn sounded, which when one is so close is deafening. Edward gave a leap backward as he was hold of Vera's hand, he nearly pulled his mother and sister over the cliff. He was shaking uncontrollably.

Vera said, "Something's happened to the little lad, Eddie. We'd better go home."

Travelling home, Edward was deathly white and still shaking.

Vera said, "Call in at the doctor's."

Dr. Alexander at Ayton swore and said, "What have you brought him out for? He has pneumonia."

They explained they had not brought him out but were already out. He gave him an injection and aspirins to take. But his condition deteriorated the next day. The doctor was sent for; he came but very reluctantly, as the cottage was only approached by a narrow winding lane and then up a winding a river. Although not deep, it had a shingle bottom. There was an alternative—up a field but it was farmed by Vera's family, who allowed no one to go up the fields but themselves. On arrival the doctor said his condition was so bad he did not expect him to see the night out. A great shock for Vera, who twenty four hours earlier had happy, healthy, four-year-old full of life and vigour.

The doctor said if he lived past mid night the worst would be over. Vera and her two-year-old daughter kept watch by the still, ashen form, so small and precious.

Vera's father came up to the strangely silent bedroom from the farm. He took one look at the delicate form.

"Oh, he's gone," and fled from the bedroom.

Next came Vera's mother. "Dad says he's gone. Oh, he has." And away she fled.

Along came Lilian, "They say he's gone. Is that right?"

"No. He is very ill, but still alive," replied Vera.

Looking at the bed Lilian said, "Oh, he has gone." And she disappeared.

The tiny two-year-old sister crept up to her mum and putting her hand on Mum's said, "He hasn't gone, Mam, 'cos I's prayin for him."

The wee fellow did recover only to fall victim to pneumonia again at seven years old. His great delight was cars, so Vera always let him sit in the front with his dad. On this occasion they were waiting at the level crossing at Seamer Junction for a train. As the gates had closed, it went through right against the car. It blew its whistle, Edward shot down onto the car floor with a yell.

Vera coaxed him out, but he was pale and trembling, so they called at the doctor who examined him and said he had pneumonia again. and should not be out.

They took him home and put him to bed, where he lived, but only through his mother's prayers.

The Hackness Vicar, the Rev. Wrigley, got Vera a job helping in the school canteen so she could keep an eye on her son while he was at school until he grew stronger. The cook was Peggy Emmerson, who later married Alan Wood. Vera and Peggy had a great rapport and Vera was very happy until Peggy married and left and a new cook from Scarborough was appointed—who had taking ways not in great things but did not mind taking a little left over school dinner for her husband's tea.

There were two girls who went to the school who were not strong children, either mentally or physically. The then headmistress, Miss Jennings, had little sympathy with a weakly child and many was the time when they heard the head telling these children they could not leave the table until their dinner was eaten. The child would be distressed and crying; there was a partition between top class and the dining room. It was wood at the bottom and glass at the top. Peggy would take a cloth and go to the tables nearest the partition and pretend to wipe the tables down while looking out of her eye corner to see were the head teacher was. Vera would come in on her hands and knees with a used plate and exchange it for the delicate child's full plate.

Vera's son went down with pneumonia again as with the other three times, all caused by shock. The third time, someone fired a gun at the back of the hedge as Vera was taking him and his sister to school. Vera looked in horror as the colour drained from her boy's face and the shaking started. She knew the telltale signs too well by now. This time he was nine-years-old and was sent to hospital. He responded to treatment although the penicillin brought him out in a rash, and he was transferred to the Cross Lane isolation hospital.

The brother and sister had never been parted before. During his stay in hospital someone gave him a tin of sweets. He ate half of those and then when anyone gave him sweets, he ate half and put half in the tin to bring his sister. Living in an isolated cottage, they never saw many sweets. They were a great treat.

He was heartbroken when he came out of the hospital, they would not let him bring the sweets with him. He said if only they had told him sooner, he could have eaten them himself. On returning home he found his devoted sister had got her dad to bring home every newspaper he could find, and she had cut out every article or picture of cars out for him. He always had a great love for motor vehicles.

Vera realising her bairns might want to farm when they got older—as farming was on both sides of the family—started her own campaign to save to buy them a farm. As they were going down the lane to school, if she heard a rabbit start to scream.

She knew a weasel, or a stoat, had got it and it would not be badly damaged. She would leave her bike with the children and race up the field to relieve it of its prey and come back with her prize, as these were her brothers and sisters' fields. She left instructions if they came by, her children had not to tell them where she was. They never did come by, but the children often wondered if they had what would they have said. Vera would take the rabbit home and dress it and bike into Scarborough with it—all for three and sixpence.

A new chef came to Hackness Hall and was in the post office one day talking to Bessie and her Aunt, Miss Hubbard, who owned and operated the wee shop. He was asking how he could obtain some blackberries. Vera was in the shop and saw potential and in an instant said she would pull him some. They agreed on a price, then he said they must be the very biggest and best—no seedy small ones, being for Lord and Lady Derwent.

Vera would have realised this anyway. A delighted Vera set to work. Fingers sore and scratched, she dutifully picked the brambles carefully, selecting all the large juicy ones to grace his Lord and Ladyship's table.

Eddie delivered them each day and asking did he require any more.

"Oh yes, as many as you can get."

Her brothers and sisters would not let her pick them in their fields. By law they could not stop her as they were only tenants themselves, but Vera did not want any unpleasantness and knew there was plenty of blackberries about. Although Eddie did gather them out of their fields before they were up on a morning, Vera went to great lengths to pick the finest blackberries, sorting through them, and only sending the big lush ones for Lord and Lady Derwent at the Hall. Using the smaller substandard ones for jelly and jam herself, at the same time thinking what a wonderful appetite for blackberries they must have.

Some weeks after all this picking and sorting for these choice fruits, the chef was not there when Eddie took the prized fruits. He explained to a member of staff the nature of his errand.

"Oh, that's were he's getting them from. They are not for his Lordship. He makes them into wine for himself."

This was heartbreaking for Vera. Not only after finding him all the most luscious fruits, but Vera was a total abstainer and would not touch wines or alcohol with a barge pole. Lowdales Farm fields surrounded Lowdales Cottage and the farm and cottage were in the bottom of the valley and the fields went up from them. Then the fields joined the Estate Woods.

Vera used to walk up to the woods and find two large branches that the foresters had cut from the bottom of the trees, then pile smaller ones on top until she had a great pile; then getting hold of the two large bottom ones and pull them down to the cottage to make bundles of kindling to start the fire on a morning. Rosie told her she could not cross their fields as she was damaging the grass, when in actual fact the grass was not marked. Farmers put heavy harrows over grass to get moss and such out and improve it, so anything a few branches did would be beneficial.

Eddie saw Mr. Butt, the agent, and explained the situation.

"Eddie, your wife is helping to stop a fire hazard. No way will she be stopped."

Vera used to crack them up and make them into bundles. She always had a hundred and fifty bundles put away in the summer, so they were dry for winter use.

As mentioned before the hens were in a large run in one of the cottage paddocks. Occasionally one would find a way out, but this was not encouraged because of the foxes. The paddock was surrounded by the farm fields. One hen in particular had found a way out of the run and was obviously was not satisfied with the paddock either, for all of a sudden there was a very loud "Vera! Vera!"

Vera rushed to the door expecting to see a disaster only to see Rosie at the gate. "You have got a hen in our field."

Vera couldn't believe her ears. What damage was a hen going to do on over two hundred acres. Vera explained that quite simply they could not find where she was getting out and wanted her in the run for her own safety.

Nearly every day was a repeat of the "Vera! Vera! and sister was there again. One day Eddie was in the house when "Vera! Vera!"

"What's that?"

So Vera quickly explained what was happening.

"Oh," he said to Vera and the bairns putting on his Wellingtons. "Vera's coming." And went out the house to the gate.

Never was anyone more dropped on to see Eddie marching up to the gate and never did anyone go so fast down the lane with a volley of broken English following her.

Vera was thrilled if she found a lemonade bottle down the road; these were glass and there was a three pence refund on returned empties. These all went into Vera's farm fund. There was money for rose hips and she pulled pounds of them. The post office would contact her if any telegrams had to be delivered to isolated farms and she did relief posting at holidays—sometimes on her bicycle but walking if the going was rough. It provided a little more income. All this after building her father and mother, brothers and sisters up to a five hundred acre farm and then being thrown out just because she got married, even though it was to a well-respected local farmer.

One year she was heartbroken to have to leave her two children on Christmas Eve. Vera always put so much into Christmas but got the chance to deliver the mail. When she got home, she got the shock of her life. Seldom did anyone do anything for Vera and when she got home, Eddie had killed the Christmas dinner and her two little ones, one not nine the other not seven, had dressed the bird.

Vera always gave the post lady, Gertie Nesfield, a cup of tea and a bit of home baking as she had a sixteen mile round, which she did on bike and foot. While having a cuppa one morning she asked Vera not to make her a cup on the following day as she would have an inspector with her and should not be stopping for a break as it was not allowed. Vera duly obliged but was surprised to hear a knock on the door.

Opening it she saw Gertie the post lady with a very tired and weary inspector.

"Oh, Mrs. Stonehouse," she said.

"I wonder if I could possibly ask you a great favour. Would you be so kind as to make this gentleman a cup of tea? He has to accompany me today and is finding it hard work. He is worn out."

"Oh, come in." Vera soon had the kettle boiling and scones buttered. Next day the post lady was laughing her head off she told Vera she was going around with the inspector and he was not up to the agricultural terrain. Uphill and down dale, and he kept saying, "Is there anywhere we can get a cup of tea?"

Eventually Gertie said, "There is just one lady I think would make a cup of tea. I'll ask her."

Vera missed her active involvement with the Gospel Assemblies and the Methodist Chapels though she walked up to Silpho Chapel on a Sunday afternoon and played the organ. She enjoyed this, although it was an uphill walk going. It was downhill returning home and was about two miles—a lovely walk up the wood which in springtime full of primroses, dog violets, anemones, bluebells, ferns, and sorrel.

When through the wood and into the open fields there was an abundance of cowslips, there was also an old quarry were oxslips grew. It was here that Vera met the dear Methodists who travelled from Scarborough to come to preach and others to drive the preachers if they had no car. One of Vera's favourites was Mr. Robbie Boyes, who always gave Vera and family a welcome when they went into town to his well-known store.

There was Mr. Nendick and Mr. Appleby and Mr. Lee. Mr. Lee loved to tell the story about when he was going to sing at a chapel with his friend. Mr. Lee was very tall and sang bass, his friend quite small and sang tenor; they had been going in at the door when they heard two young lads say, "It is funny little un sings up and big un sings doon."

Vera sadly missed her singing around the various places of worship, and she so missed her involvement in the Sunday School anniversaries. At the anniversaries there was a service in the afternoon where the children would recite poems, sing solos, and choir pieces they had spent weeks practising. Every piece was to learn by heart. No one was allowed to read them.

Although it was a long walk to Silpho, Vera would sometimes take her children with her. If she did, after the service there was a high light for them. Mr. and Mrs. Jack Hunter would have them in for cup of tea. Mrs. Hunter's little cottage was beautiful, the furniture highly polished and the brass gleamed in the flickering firelight. Hours must have been spent lovingly caring for the wonderful home. A roaring fire in black leaded grate the hearth plate rested on a large stone flag beautifully stoned with donkey brick, graced with gleaming brass fire irons (poker, brush and small dustpan).

Mr. Hunter had a garden so well-tended, not a weed to be seen and row upon row of healthy vegetables in straight lines beans and peas running up canes. All lovingly netted to stop birds stealing the precious produce a pond was just outside the cottage with ducks swimming on it.

The infant teacher at Hackness School started a competition—which child could bring the most wildflowers of different species. The teacher was frequently going to Vera in the canteen, such was Vera's love and knowledge of wildflowers. There were a few arguments when a certain child had brought a flower and their mum had said it was so and so. Vera would say it definitely wasn't, and it would result in Vera having to take a flower book to prove her point.

Vera was well read and loved reading when she could find time. She lent a lady from the neighbouring village of Broxa a particular book. She could not get it back, always a different excuse was given. Vera was telling the post mistress at the Post Office, Bessie Robinson, who asked Vera what the book was called. When Vera told her, "Oh," she said, "I have that. It's been all round the village." And that was the village of Hackness as well as Broxa.

Vera said, "Please give me it back when you have finished with it. It is one of a series and I have them all." When it was handed back it had a shopping list written inside the cover.

Eddie had lovely manners but when Vera and Eddie were going out in the car, if the road was gated, Vera would always get out and open the gates as Eddie was driving. It saved him having to get out to open the gate and get back in drive through and get out again to shut it; most farmers wives did the same. Vera had a friend, Phyllis from Bury St. Edmunds, came to stay. They were going for a ride, so Vera got into the back of the two door Ford Anglia. They got to the first gate; Eddie had to put car out of gear and brake on get out open gate get in same procedure to close the gate. There were a lot of gated roads in the country in the 1940s to 1950s; this happened at every gate until they reached their destination. When they were ready to return home, Phyllis stood back to let Vera get into the back.

Eddie, seeing this, said, "Just a minute, Phyllis, are you going to open the gates?"

"No, definitely not. I would never open a gate for a man."

"Right then, you get in the back."

Mr. and Mrs. Nesfield who were neighbours when Vera was at Woodhouse had a married daughter, Doris, and her husband, Wardie, who lived at Highdales near Lowdales at Hackness. They had a farm at Harwood Dale but had moved off in the war years as it was next to the military's Low North Camp. Although Wardie kept his sheep on and had to walk over every day to see them.

Wardie did not drive a car; they were about two miles away from Vera. They had to use the same road to Hackness and both families either walked or cycled so they met a lot. Their children were the same ages and they became lifelong friends. When Doris was expecting their youngest child, Wardie said to Eddie he was worried about having to go for the nurse and leave Doris, especially if baby should come at night.

So Eddie said, "I'll take the car up home, come for me, and I'll go for the nurse."

There were no telephones in the area. One night Vera and Eddie had gone to bed and Vera, unable to sleep, saw a light flashing on the bedroom wall. She said, "Eddie, get up. Wardie's coming."

She shot out of bed and shouted from the window "It's all right, Wardie. Eddie's going for nurse, you go back to Doris."

"Thank you, Mrs. Eddie." Wardie's favourite name for Vera.

Next day Vera put the oven on and baked a basket of food and took it up to Wardie and Doris in their hour of need. A gift that must have been returned hundreds of times over as a more generous couple could not be found than Wardie and Doris.

Eddie worked on the Estate at Hackness and gave Vera a pound a week, out of which she clothed and fed the family and ran the car, thinking, Eddie was only keeping a bit of pocket money for himself. One day he was not well, and the post mistress gave Vera the wage envelope which the Estate had left for him at the post office, asking her to take it to Eddie when she came from the school. Written on the outside was £3.10. Realisation dawned; he had been giving her £1 to keep the family on and he had £2.10s for pocket money.

With Eddie having stomach problems and having a sweet tooth, Vera saved her sweet ration, too, and gave it to Eddie. He loved chocolate; so when they went shopping, Vera bought him the blocks of Cadbury's Chocolate; being solid chocolate and not having fancy fillings, they lasted longer. When Edward started eating, she thought it was time he was having some sweets. She broke a few pieces off a bar and gave him some leaving some pieces on the end of the table. She went out to do something and when she came back Eddie had been in and the chocolate gone.

A few days later he come in and said, "I think I'll get my own sweets in future. Can I have my coupons?"

"Yes, I'll fetch them." And she gave him his own coupons, not hers which he had been eating. "Now be careful. These coupons have to last you a month."

They went shopping and when they got back to the car, Eddie was eating away. She noticed as they were going home, he was eating Frys cream bars which of course melt in the mouth and don't last as long as the solid blocks of chocolate. Whenever she saw him that night he was "chew! chew! chew!" Next day at dinner time he came into the house and said, "How long did you say those coupons had to last me?"

"A month," Vera replied.

"Well it's all gone."

"What?" Vera said. "In one day?"

"Yes, but you get me more than that."

"Yes, because you have been eating mine and the bairns ration as well. You thought when you saw it on the table, I was giving him yours, but I wasn't. It was his own ration. You have been eating his."

"Well," he said, "I'll let you get mine in future." A lesson well learned.

Vera loved Christmas and worked hard to make it a special occasion for the children. Normally in the evening the living room was lit with a paraffin lamp with one wick. Now if there is a power cut in the electricity supply and the paraffin lamp is lit, we can hardly see anything as the eyes are so used to the bright light. Vera had the Tilley lamps and the Aladdin, but they had the mantles instead of wicks and used a lot more paraffin, so they only came out at Christmas.

Vera sat up late in the evening sewing by the side of the one wick paraffin lamp. She kept her old dresses and made these into pretty dresses and matching hair bands for her daughter and the plain colours into little shirts for her son.

One year about a week after Christmas, while going home one morning having taken the children to school, Vera was cycling and catching up on a horse drawn cart going in the same direction as she was. Looking at the load, she soon realised it was a going to the local tip from Hackness Hall. Looking at the cart, she saw a lot of Christmas decorations. As soon as the cart delivered its load, Vera was in filling her cycle basket with the most beautiful streamers, globes, candle holders, Chinese lanterns, and fairy lights. She had no electricity but cut the cables off the lights which were lovely Chinese designs with brightly coloured tassels. When Vera tied these with pretty cords, they made lovely hangings for the tree for over fifty years, and still some of the items from Vera's treasure trove are loved dearly by the family.

Vera went to great lengths for her children on Christmas Eve. She always prepared the bird for the oven, peeled the potatoes, and prepared the sprouts, so she could spend as much time as possible watching the bairns open their presents on Christmas Day. Looking back there was never any presents for Vera. Only Gertie the post lady used to bring her hankies or perfume and her friend from Bury St. Edmunds sent a little something, but she never complained. Everything was geared up for her children. In the morning after the stockings—which were the cloth bags that flour came in at that time, washed out and pressed—were opened always the tangerine, sweets and coins in the bottom, books for both, little toys and tools for Edward and sewing and knitting sets for Sylvia. A lovely dinner of chicken and all the trimmings and a scrumptious homemade pudding with white sauce was cooked. Vera made her own ginger wine, peppermint cordial, and one drink made from oranges and another from lemons. The afternoon was spent quietly usually reading. That and Sundays were the only times Vera had to relax. She never allowed any work to be done in her home on the Lord's Day, other than preparing meals and feeding any animals—something her children have kept in their own homes. Vera always made her own Christmas cake and pork pie with numerous other goodies for tea. Weeks before Christmas, Vera would start making sweets: fondant, coconut ice, peppermint creams, and Turkish delight.

Christmas Day was always kept sacred; there were no games until Boxing Day. Although stockings and presents were opened and Christmas dinner with all the trimmings, a hand reared plump juicy bird was enjoyed.

Vera purchased day old chicks. They usually came in boxes to the railway station at Scarborough. Vera put them in brooders with paraffin lamps to keep them warm. The warm chicks and the paraffin lamps produced an unusual not unpleasant smell that could be remembered for years. The pullets were kept for laying hens but the cockerills were reared for Christmas—one being kept for the family, the rest Vera plucked and dressed and took to customers in Scarborough.

The bird Vera kept was served with home cured bacon on its breast stuffed with stuffing from Vera's recipe of marjoram suet and breadcrumbs. It was always made with local marjoram grown by Mr. Longhorn from Wrench Green. Most people made stuffing from sage but not Vera. This was cooked in lard from Vera's own pig, all served with her own bread sauce and Yorkshire puddings that hit the oven roof. Roast potatoes and sprouts grown by Vera in her own garden followed with homemade puddings and white sauce. The children always loved it when in the autumn Vera would say I'm going to make the Christmas puddings tonight. Mixing bowls would come out and dried fruit washed. An old sheet torn up for pudding cloths. The puddings duly made, put into the cloths, and boiled, then drained and hung in hooks in the kitchen. Once the puddings were hung it really did feel as if Christmas was not too far away.

On Boxing Day, Vera had a few jobs to catch up with. Always having hens and animals, at Lowdales it was a pig, a cow, a pony, a dog, and cat, so there was always something to do. Eddie did not like visitors. So it was a quiet day. The bairns always felt dinner was a bit of a letdown after the sumptuous fare of the previous day. It was a case of eating yesterday's leftovers as it was just after the war and food stuffs still scarce. The juicy bird was now cold and the crisp roast potatoes were exchanged for the jacket taties that were cooked with the bird, which were now fried the Yorkshire puddings, were noticeable by their absence; but there was always plenty to eat. In the evening, Vera tried her best to make it special. She had a large store of party games. The Aladdin lamp was allowed to be lit, giving a better light and games were played, such as "I'm the Barrel Organ Man". All players would have to play a pretend musical instrument. Vera would be the Barrel Organ Man, and all would sing "I'm the Barrel Organ Man, I'm the Barrel Organ man, I'll do all that ever I can, cause I'm the barrel Organ Man." When the barrel organ man switched to your instrument you had to play the barrel organ if you failed to notice you were out.

Then there was the "Parsons Hen Roost". Vera would start the tale making it up as she went on about a parson that had a hen roost and somebody stole a hen, and all players would have been given a different line to say such as: "I plucked it", "I stole it", "I ate it". When Vera asked you what you did you had only to say your line. It was her job to make you say something else if you did you were out.

"There was a parson had a hen roost one night. Someone broke in and stole a hen. Do you know anything about it?

"I ate it." But it had its feathers on, "I ate it."

It had its insides still in "I ate it" etc.

Then turning to the next player "Do you know anything about it?"

"I cooked it." But it had its feathers on, "I cooked it."

Vera had a great fund of pencil games too, although all cereal boxes were made into spills to light lamps and stoves from the fire, she used to keep some of them to write on at Christmas time. Vera also had a great many tricks and puzzles with matches, coins, and buttons.

Vera's home grown vegetables would have won her many an accolade if she had frequented village shows, but she was always too busy. Her children had many happy hours playing hide-and-seek up the potato rows. Vera never complained, even after all her hard work digging and weeding and planting.

Yet Eddie would be extremely mad if they went anywhere near the hay sheds. Although Vera had her own pig and poultry. These were chiefly for supplying customers, not for family use.

Chapter 13

SAWDON A DISAPPOINTMENT MADE GOOD

EDDIE'S MOTHER RENOVATED HER UNCLE Jacksie's dilapidated farmhouse in Sawdon Village and told Eddie he could have it for a similar rent to Lowdales. Eddie was impressed as he had two married sisters living in the village, his mother and a cousin. His relatives on his mother's side had farmed and owned land at Sawdon for many years.

Vera was not so pleased; although, always one for broadening her horizons, she remembered it had been demolished during the renovation, leaving property very difficult to make comfortable. It had running hot and cold water. The water was heated by a back boiler from a Rayburn cooker which would go out rather than ignite. It was a problem to keep it burning; consequently, water for baths and such were still heated with a large kettle.

The house did have a bathroom and electricity, which the Lowdales had not. The living room was very small and had seven doors. It would have made a good entrance hall but not a room to live in. Vera was able to get a sideboard in but not a table. There was no room for a suite or comfortable chairs, only upright dining or kitchen chairs could be used. In this room there was a door leading to the small drawing room which could have been made a little more comfortable had it not housed the dining table and everything that would not fit in elsewhere.

There was a door up the stairs, the back door, front door, kitchen and bathroom doors, and a door under the stairs, and a full length door on a cupboard housing the electricity meter. This could have been outside in a shed, but no it was in a built in a cupboard about five feet high and six inches deep. On the front wall there was the front door. This cupboard and a large window were on the south wall. A door into the drawing room and a fireside were on the west wall. There was a door leading under the stairs cupboard. The back door was on the north wall, plus the bathroom and kitchen door. There was no wall space to stand anything against. Eddie did not mind but Vera and the bairns despaired at that house.

The kitchen was very tiny with a built in kitchen cabinet, which took up nearly all the room. Certainly not a choice specimen, an item knocked together with hardboard. If you gave it a good wash, the hardboard lifted. It had an aluminum work surface that left your cloth black every time you washed it. There were a large sink and a rough wood draining board, a large window which nearly came down to the floor, and a very small pantry. You could not step inside it. You opened the door and could reach all the shelves.

Poor Vera remembered it as a large farmhouse. Thankfully it was the worst house Vera and family had ever lived in and the worst she ever would live in. Several times Vera would say to Eddie ask your mam if we can alter this or that.

"No. I will not. It's like finding fault."

So as far as the house was concerned, they spent six very difficult years.

On moving to Sawdon, Vera quickly made friends with the village folk; being a good cook and she exchanged many recipes and cooking hints and also baked for some of the village events.

The Lord blessed Vera at Sawdon in many ways and she was happy there—apart from the house—if not blissfully content. There were three paddocks, so she could still have her cow and poultry and make hay for the cow. Eddie and Vera exchanged the car for a van and in the evenings would pick up the extra grass when the council cut the roadside verges. They would lead it home and spread it in the yard and field and Vera would turn that and grass cut in their own hay field by hand several times a day until it was dry and made into hay.

Vera realised both her and her children wanted to go into farming. She always knew this was a possibility as it was in them from both sides, so she took on extra work. Nephew Albert Foster, who Vera thought the world of, knew Vera was saving for a farm and asked her if she would like to stook some corn for him as he and his father would like to keep cutting with the binder. Vera went not only stooking sheaves but also hoeing turnips and in winter cleaning them for Albert.

Vera never had a driving license. She could drive a tractor, but it was the only job she really disliked and rarely did it.

There was a group of men at Sawdon known as "The Gang" who in the evening after their daytime jobs were finished, used to go together to the farms to hoe turnips or stook corn—whatever the seasonal jobs were. They did some stooking for Albert, but Vera always asked if she could work in a field on her own. This was something she always did if possible, even on her own farm.

After one really stormy night Albert went up the street to tell Vera he had been to the field and only her stooks of corn were standing, not one of hers had fallen down. It was never known for any of Vera's to fall even when she was farming on her own farm. Vera always worked as hard as any man and always made a good job of anything she did.

A friend of Eddie's, George Stephenson, who managed Park Farm for Sir Paul Bryan, asked Vera if she would hoe them some turnips as there were more than "The Gang" could cope with. She said if he would mark her some rows off separately, she would hoe them. When she had finished, he came to pay her and said he walked up and down the rows she had done and never found a double, which is two turnips left growing together. If two turnips are left together, they obviously do not grow as big. George was delighted and gave her the same wage as the men.

Eddie's cousin, John Temple, was talking to Vera and remarked that they had a field of turnips that had beaten them. They had grown too big and were buried in rubbish. "The Gang" would not hoe them. Vera said she would have a go. She asked if they would scruffle (a scruffler is a machine that takes the rubbish from between the rows) a row or two before she started and then scruffled the soil back after she had hoe'd them. This procedure was done each day until Vera had finished them. It was very hard work and took a lot out of Vera. When John came to pay her, he insisted on giving Vera a man's wage as he said she had done a man's job.

Mary Skelton who lived with her brother, Henry, at the other side of Sawdon Dale, north of Ruston. Mary used to walk across the Dale to the Sawdon Methodist Chapel and to see her friend Edith Abbs. Mary said to Vera that they could do with a bit of help with the Stooking of the corn, so Vera went to give them a hand. She walked across the dale to mow their thistles. It was a long way across the dale, but Vera loved working at Henry and Mary's. She was very happy there. She was treated as one of the family, was given cups of tea, offered meals, but she could not stay as she had her own family's tea to prepare. During school holidays, Vera could take the bairns across with her and they were made very welcome and given bags of sweets.

Moving to Sawdon had its benefits and Vera could eventually see the Lord's hand in the move. Since being married she had been unable to attend her beloved Gospel Hall in Scarborough, as she never drove a car and there was only a bus service on a Thursday and Saturday from Sawdon. This was a disappointment to her, but she saw the urgent need of a Sunday School. There were quite a few children in the village, and they were unable to learn the Scriptures or the way of salvation. Vera made enquires and was given permission to start one. It was her pride and joy as she loved the children and had a great way of getting the best out of them. Although Eddie did not encourage Vera to sing and she had no transport without him to carry out any singing engagements, she had retained her beautiful singing voice and was delighted to be able to sing at the Sunday School anniversaries.

On the bus some of the passengers were discussing the forthcoming First Sunday School Anniversary, which Vera was organizing, and two categories caused more jealousy and rivalry than any other one. Singing and soloists and the other organists both come in for an abundant supply of criticism. One of the ladies on the service bus going to Scarborough was Eva Warriner—then Pearson—who had loved to hear Vera sing for many years.

A lady passenger on the bus said, "I don't know what Mrs. Stonehouse is going to do. The anniversary is on Sunday and she has never had a practice yet."

Eva said, "You what! Vera doesn't need a practice. She could sing if she stood on her head."

After one anniversary in which the Chapel was filled to capacity, Jack Dickinson from Hutton Buscel said, "Well done, Vera. That was a great credit to you."

His brother, Herbert the chapel steward, said, "Brian's superintendent you know."

"Hod thee noise," replied Jack "Thou and Brian's been here lang enough an there's never bin a Sunday school."

A great favourite of Vera's were Herbert Trousdale and his family. The children were a great joy to her. Vera had such a special way of reading to children and telling stories. She put so much into them, like wise training the children for the anniversaries. Vera would get down on her knees by the side of a small shy child that was just mumbling its recitation and point to a mark high up on the wall at the back of the chapel.

"Now just imagine that is a spider, a very deaf spider, but he wants to hear what you have to say. Look at it, don't take your eyes off it, now say each word as loud as you can."

That way the child's head was held up high, face looking above the congregation. They could hear every word and the child was not nervous looking at a sea of faces. It was natural that when a child was nervous, he looks at the ground and any sound coming from his mouth comes out as a mumble, but Vera overcame this.

Vera and Eddie went shopping to Scarborough on a Saturday. One morning Vera was getting her jobs done, children ready, eggs for sale packed, and such, when there was a knock at the door. Opening it she found an Indian with a case selling his wares and he started the usual sales patter.

Vera said she was in a hurry.

"Oh, but you will live to be ninety-three?"

"Really. But I am still in a hurry."

He kept on with his sales talk and Vera was getting more and more frustrated with him. "Eddie, can you come? I've a lot to do."

When Eddie got to the door and Vera went inside the Indian said, "My you have a bad tempered wife and don't worry she won't live to be ninety-three." The family loved this and teased Vera for years about it.

Vera and Eddie lived next door to the pub where local much-loved character, Bob Warriner—who although retired—did a few jobs there. He and Vera would have a lot of banter over the garden wall. Vera was working away in the garden when she heard the cuckoo. For a minute she stood upright then realising who it was said, "It's all right, Bob. It's the wrong time of year for the cuckoo."

Vera was very fond of Carter and Cissie Stephenson: farmers who lived on the other side. Their only son, Eric, had a war injury and was limited in what he could do. He was a great pigeon fancier, and on a Saturday, he was regularly walking up to John Temple's, Eddies cousin, who lived at Old Farm (he was another big pigeon fancier) to check on the incoming bird situation. Eric had a little grey Fergie tractor and as most of their land was outside the village, he became a familiar sight riding by with his little dog on his knee.

Vera's cousin, Albert Robson, his wife, Connie—a vicar's daughter—and their three daughters: Yvonne, Valerie, and Sonia, lived at Grove Farm. Albert's father, Alf, when Vera was young, farmed at Wansford near Driffield; as mentioned before he was sick and tired of people walking across his land. Foot paths were originally for people to get from their home to either their work or for Services or social calls. Not so many people used them for hiking or rambles. As mentioned before Driffield folk had started to go across the Robson's land for a Sunday stroll and were making the path wider and not sticking to its designated route.

This was getting Alf annoyed so one Sunday morning he sent Albert early to tar all the styles. In those days ladies all wore long dresses and climbed onto the styles sitting on the top and swinging their legs over the men could just climb and stride over the styles.

Vera's family lived in Driffield at that time and her mother wondered what all the ladies were doing shuffling by with their husbands shielding their rear. When they heard about the styles, they knew what had happened. However, it earned Albert the nick name "Tarry A".

The newspapers at Sawdon were delivered to Billy Ruston's blacksmith's shop. Vera went to pick up Eddie's paper. The blacksmiths was full of locals catching up on the local gossip including Albert. Vera picked up the paper and was walking back up the street when Albert leaning out of the door shouted, "Vera, you're getting a rare starn on you."

She turned round and yelled, "You're the last one to talk about backsides, Tarry!" He shot across the road to his house like a bullet.

Vera had dear friends at Sawdon: Joan Bielby, whose husband Fred was a man who could be relied upon and worked at Mount Pleasant Farm. Joan, like Vera, loved singing and often popped in for a chat. She suffered from asthma and passed away far too soon. Mary Temple, Eddie's cousin's wife, used to knock on the window. It was a friendly tap or a prolonged tapping if she wanted a reply and Edith Abbs also would tap on the window every time she passed, even if she had not time to call in. She lived in a remote cottage north of the village with her brothers.

A group of young men—they could not be called children even if they behaved worse—decided one night that Horace Abbs, one of Edith's brothers, would be alone in the lonely cottage. They decided to play a trick on him, a trick that could have had tragic results. They climbed on to the roof and put a wet sack over the chimney pot. The smoke could not get out and filled the room. Fortunately, Horace woke; had he not done so, he could easily have been suffocated.

The same young men took a five-barred gate off an entrance to a house south of the village and carried it up to the village pond and were just putting it in when the owner came past and recognized his gate. he made them carry it all the way back again.

Another unkind prank they played was on Carter Stephenson and his son. Carter and Eric had got a field of corn stooked, as mentioned before Eric was injured in the war so it was no easy task. During the night the pranksters moved all the sheaves and stooked them upside down in one long stook across the field. As with the rest of their pranks this was not funny as the ears of corn were drawing moisture out of the ground and had to be stooked properly immediately.

George Stephenson called to pay Vera for some work, and it was mentioned that for the first time the family would not have their own Christmas tree.

"Oh, don't worry about a tree. I'll drop you one off when I get ours."

Christmas Eve came and no tree. Vera always liked hers decorated a week before Christmas. At teatime, Vera was really worried; then there was a knock on the door and in came George with no Christmas tree and never even mentioned one.

When he'd gone, Vera went out in the dark and came back with a huge branch of holly she'd sawn from a tree in her field and planted in a bucket.

It was a bit prickly to decorate but was very effective and looked lovely. Vera could always find a way round any problem. Years later when there was a family party the lawn mower broke down. It was a huge lawn, but as well as baking, cleaning, and doing everything associated with a party at home, Vera cut the lawn with a pair of kitchen scissors.

The family never had holidays, but occasionally Eddie would take Vera and family to see dear friends Wardie and Doris Nesfield and their family at High Langdale End or Harry Riby and his sisters at Harwood Dale. Harry worked for Eddie's father for many years and was always fond of Eddie.

Eddie knowing Vera was working hard and saving every penny for a farm, not only doing without luxuries but often essentials for herself. Instead of the usual ride out to Harwood Dale, he said, "I am taking you for a ride somewhere else." And took the family to Egton Bridge and Rosedale Abbey, then up the lovely valley of Hartoft.

Looking across the valley he asked, "What do you think of that farm?"

"Why?" asked Vera

"It's for sale," replied Eddie.

On returning home. Vera asked her children—then thirteen and eleven years old—what they thought of it.

Both enthusiastically replied that they loved it. Eddie said it was not vacant. There was a tenant on it, but the Keldy Castle Estate was being sold and this was one of the farms on it. The estate being owned at that time by the Ministry of Agriculture.

Vera wrote off for details and permission to view. On viewing the tenant was really encouraging, "Don't put your money in this place, Mrs. It grows nothing but stones."

On mentioning turnips, "You'll not grow turnips up here, Mrs. They only grow as big as marbles."

Saying that she wanted to keep some sheep, "You'll never get twins. There's only singles born up here."

It was a hill farm on the north York, moors at the edge of the Cropton Forest. Vera put in an offer which she asked her family to pray about it. Vera never did anything on her own initiative, always took everything to the Lord in prayer. The ministry accepted her offer; Vera was delighted she now had a farm, but it would enable her son to finish his education. He was doing very well at Scarborough Boys High School which was then at Westwood.

Two years later there was a knock on Vera's door at Sawdon. There was the tenant, "My son-in-law has left me; and I can't manage. I have brought a letter with a name and address of someone who's willing to take it off your hand."

Vera and Eddie talked it over. Vera went to the Boys High School to see the headmaster who was reluctant to release Edward, but Edward said he would rather go farming than go through college. Vera realised if she let it again it would not be available when she wanted it.

Vera knew she had to take the farm on herself. Cousin John Temple and his son, Robin, were good advisors—having a wealth of recent farming knowledge. They took Vera to farm sales to purchase a tractor and trailer, corn drill and root drill, turnip cutter and other things dealing with farming. Being out of farming for so long everything was bought from scratch, both in small tools and large.

The pub next door to Vera at Sawdon changed hands and there was a sale. Vera was able to buy some furniture for her farm and house there. She had worked so hard and saved every penny for so many years for this farm and yet the loving mother never left her. Her children knew not to ask for anything. They learnt at an early age their mother was saving for a farm for them and was having to work well past her strength; yet at the sale there was a box of jewelry. Noticing her daughter looking at it longingly, but not saying anything, she bought it for her.

Chapter 14

HEAD HOUSE FARM

ON THE APRIL 6, 1959, Vera moved to Head House Farm, Hartoft, near Pickering with a fifteen year old son and thirteen year old daughter, a load of calves, and twelve pounds in her pocket. Eddie had not Vera's courage and decided to keep the house at Sawdon in case poor Vera failed. After all, he still had a mother and two sisters at Sawdon. Hartoft was not far from Sawdon—a distance of about 26 miles—and Eddie went up to the farm on weekends as Vera had not a license to drive. Edward was not old enough to drive on the road and they needed to go shopping.

Hartoft is a pretty moorland valley of outlying farms and cottages. There were small holdings which were homes for the forestry workers, where they could keep a cow and some poultry and a few young beast. They had about eight acres.

A man from the Ministry of Agriculture was in a public house in Pickering one Monday Market Day when he overheard a Hartoft farmer say, "What's a woman want bringing two bairn's tiv a farm like that."

Mr. Stone replied, "She will maybe show you a thing or two."

"Dis thou know her?"

"Yes. I have known her and her family for years."

The valley was all down to grass being predominantly a moor sheep area and when Vera got a few sheep she had plenty of twins born. She always looked well after them and got the sheep inside for lambing.

The land was productive and did grow corn and turnips. A farm sale was held at a neighbouring holding and the neighbours, taking a short cut across Vera's fields, were amazed to see the good size of the turnips.

After a few years, Vera said one night, "I've got a feeling I have to buy Birch House."

Which was the next farm up the valley and it had a tenant on it. The family could not understand it.

"Why is it for sale?" Her son and daughter asked.

"I don't know but pray about it. I will write tomorrow and find out."

A short time later an auctioneer contacted Vera, "How did you know Birch House was for sale?"

"I don't know," she replied.

"Well, I've never known anything like it. I have just received two letters. One from the Ministry wanting us to sell Birch House and your letter wanting to buy it."

Vera did purchase it; later she was to buy the land from High Farm which was farmed in conjunction with Head House. It was very fertile land and grew plentiful crops. Vera had a grain silo erected and was now virtually self-sufficient.

Two years passed at Hartoft without a car. Eddie came up on weekends but still had no desire to live there. He said, "Oh, they'll be back before eighteen months is up."

"We've been up there over two years already," replied Edward.

Eddie felt his mother needed him at Sawdon and being born near Scarborough and farming there for nearly forty years, he had no desire to move to a "moor farm" for longer than weekends. He also hated farm work and used to say, "I will come up a bit later while you're hay making and then you will get finished."

When purchased by Vera, Head House had no electricity or running hot water and the road was on poor state of repair. All these were rectified by Vera in the first few years.

Shortly after arriving at Head House, a plan was afoot to bring electricity to the valley. There were meetings in Pickering to try and assess how many in were in favour; it was discovered the majority living in the dale were very much for it. Quite a few farms were still owned by the Ministry of Agriculture. Mr. Rowntree from the Ministry came to see Vera and gave her some sound advice. He was related to a family Vera knew when she was at Hackness. Some of the men from the Ministry, their advice had to be taken with a pinch of salt as it was said that some were "broken down farmers", in other words they at one time had been farmers and could not make farming pay and had to leave their farms, and then got jobs advising those who were making a living how to farm.

Mr. Rowntree always gave sound and helpful advice. He told Vera about the small farmers' scheme which was on the go. There were grants on farm buildings and roads and improving the land as well as subsidies on cattle. This was spread over several years. Mr. Rowntree was amazed when Vera said she wanted a combined dutch barn, cattle shed, and implement shed erecting first.

"But what about modernising the house?"

"Oh," she said, "We can do that when we have some cattle in the sheds to pay for it."

The agricultural building was erected, and the old stable made into calf pens. The house eventually did get electricity and a bathroom; there were no luxuries as this was a working farm and Vera meant that it should pay its way.

Next on the agenda was the road. It crossed a valley and heavy rains ran down it, so it was no economy job. As the tenants of the forestry holding above Head House used the road, Vera approached the Forestry Commission, with whom she always got on with very well, asking if they would help to pay for the mending of the road.

"If our tenants are using it, then yes there's no problem."

Vera was walking her daughter across the valley to school one morning when the tenant approached her. He was with a group of forestry workers planting trees. He was very unpleasant to Vera, shouting at her that he did not use the road and wanted nothing to do with it.

"But," Vera said, "You do use it. Your wife uses it every morning and evening to take your children to the school bus and collect them."

He shouted and raged at Vera. She could not understand it, as the men working with him were local and could see him and his wife using the road. It was the Forestry Commission that was willing to pay; it was not going to cost him a penny.

Vera got a letter from the forestry saying their tenant said he did not use the road therefore they would not help to meet the cost. Vera went ahead and had a lovely tarmac road made with money she could ill afford. She could not believe her eyes when no sooner had the tarmac lorries and road rollers disappeared than the tenant's wife came through with the children to the school bus and back again.

Vera immediately phoned the Forestry Commission and asked them what they advised.

"Mrs. Stonehouse, as far as we are concerned, you can build a wall across we do not need access."

Vera told them she would not do that if it could be helped, as it was the forestry's nearest way to the river for water if there was a forest fire. The next morning the wife went through with the children again and when she returned a farm trailer was in the gateway. She had to turn round and go back through the forestry, their official road. That week Vera was at a sale of farm implements and machinery; the husband came up to her and started shouting and mouthing it off about not being able to use Vera's road. Vera tried to explain that all he had had to do was tell the forestry he used the road and they would have helped pay for it and he and his family could have continued to use it.

He was shouting and waving his arms in rage when a voice at the side of Vera said, "Are you all right, Mrs. Stonehouse?"

There at her side was Mr. Farrow, the scrap metal dealer. She thanked him and said she was all right, but no sooner had she got the words out than a large lorry pulled up at her other side. It was one Jacob Foster's men, another renowned scrap metal dealer.

Terry leaned out of the window, "Are you all right, Mrs. Stonehouse?"

"Thank you, Terry, I'm fine." Vera never forgot those gentlemen and their great kindness, concern, and their high regard for her. When she arrived home, Vera phoned the Forestry Commission and they said they would send a man out to assess the situation.

It was hay time. It was loose hay no bales then and Vera was forking hay onto the elevator. Sylvia was forking it to Edward who was stacking it. Being high up on the stack, he looked up and saw these rather nice cars and Land Rovers park at the top of the field. A man amongst several others got out. He was wearing a smart suit. The man Vera had been dealing with at the Forestry Headquarters was a Mr. Murdoch. Edward had a great sense of fun. He leaned over the side of the stack and told his mam that the man from the forestry was coming.

"Remember, Mam, it's Mr. Burdoch."

When the group came through the gate, Vera went across to meet them. Going up to the man in the suit, who held out his hand, Vera shook hands with him and said, "You'll be Mr. Bur . . . Mr. Mur . . . Mr. Bur . . . Mr. Murgatroyd?"

There was peals of mirth echoed from the top of the stack. When normality resumed, he stressed the tenant had told them he did not use the road, but once again he said a wall could be built across the road stopping all access.

The water supply was pumped up the hill to the farm by a hydraulic ram from a spring of water. It was ample, but if it wanted to break down. It always chose the coldest day of the year. Edward would stand in the chamber of the ram, fiddling with valves, while his mother or sister stood by and nearly perished keeping an eye on him, seeing he did not succumb to the bitter elements. They were also used as "go-fors": go for a piece of wire, go for a smaller screwdriver or a larger pair of pliers.

One really hot day before the dutch barn was built, the family were making hay. Edward had brought a sweep of hay to the bottom of the elevator which stood beside the stack. He was about to start the elevator. No one was near the tractor when the engine started revving like mad. The tractor was rocking, and steam was belching out from her.

Ed shouted, "Run for it! She'll blow up!"

"What's happened?" said Vera.

"Governor rods blown off. She will get that hot and she will explode."

Thinking of her winter fodder going up in flames and not being able to afford another tractor, Vera with her usual cry of "Pray for me" ran up to the red hot tractor yelling, "What am I looking for?"

"A piece of narrow pipe about four inches long."

Bending down near the tractor, she ran her fingers in the hay and grass and picked up the offending article, shouting, "Where does it go?"

Edward then darted forward and stuck it on. Once more normality was restored and Vera's loving Heavenly Father upheld her and her faith in Him once more and protected her from all danger. No wonder Vera could always say, "The Lord is so good to me."

A man from the ministry came to see the dutch barn, fold yard, and implement shed unit to see if it was erected to the correct standards before the grant was paid. The field beyond the stack yard where the unit was built was slightly uphill and Vera and Edward stood in this field with the sheep grazing around them, discussing the building when the ministry man was suddenly projected several yards in front of them on the head of the ram.

Cleaning turnips was a chilling enterprise as it was always done in winter months usually by Vera. It was nothing new to see Vera on the coldest days in winter up in the turnip field pulling and cleaning the turnips with no gloves or stockings on. At that time, she just did not have the money for gloves and stockings; they were luxuries to Vera and there were no fancy Barbour waterproof jackets and trousers for the hill farmers then. On one day of heavy rain, Vera had thirteen wet coats.

Although no money for fancy work attire, Vera was always well dressed when she went out no matter if it was to the Gospel Hall, chapel, farm sale, cattle market or shopping. She always had a smart coat, hat, and gloves—even on a hot summer's day. Vera carried a nice handbag and gloves. This she always did from being a young girl until the last time she went out to a choir practice at the age of a hundred years.

Vera went into milk production; one year there were heavy frosts for many days. The turnips were frozen into the ground. Vera realised with the cows not having the turnips they loved, the milk production would drop dramatically, as turnips are ninety nine per cent water. She took the pickaxe to the field and got the turnips out of the ground, one for each cow. They were then thrown on a cart and delivered to the cow house and put in rows at the back were the cows warm breath thawed them for next day. Vera did this every day until the frosts went.

To reach Head House, as already mentioned, a valley had to be crossed. Quite steep, Edward parked the tractor and trailer on the grass by the side of the road facing downhill while taking turnips to a field of cattle. Vera, her son, and daughter all climbed onto the trailer and, as they were throwing the turnips off, it was never known if the extra movement of the throwing off the turnips released it but somehow the brake was released, and tractor and trailer went careering down the hill.

Edward as cool as a cucumber said, "She's off and I can't do a thing about it."

Vera, after her arrow prayers to her beloved Lord, yelled, "Jump clear!"

All three jumped at the same time and her dear Lord provided a large stone which the tractor hit, turning the wheels into the ditch instead of hurtling down the road. Sylvia missed her footing on landing and fell into the same ditch. Vera, although herself well clear, saw the still loaded trailer toppling over and in the blink of an eye ran underneath and dragged her daughter out of danger.

Vera had a Boythorpe crop store built. There was always some corn left at the bottom that the auger couldn't reach; so opening the little side door, she climbed in and started to shovel up the corn into bags and throw it out. She was working away when she suddenly started to feel bit funny, but thinking it was the heat of the day or the exertion she tried to keep going. Knowing something serious was the matter, she struggled to the little door and managed to climb out then collapsed. She managed to get to her feet but felt awful. She struggled to the field were her daughter was harrowing and said she felt dreadful.

Sylvia took her home and made her a cup of tea. Vera was never a doctor person and was quite ill for some days. It was found out that poisonous gasses build up in the crop stores and several farmers had been killed by entering them. No one should go in without them being thoroughly ventilated and then not on their own. Someone must be outside and keeping an eye on the person or persons cleaning them out. Once again Vera's Lord was watching over her.

The top fields at Head House, which joined the forestry, started to hold a lot of water. The Forestry Commission had planted a lot of trees and Vera thought they had blocked the natural drainage. Turnips being grown in the field were under water and going rotten. It was getting worse, so Vera contacted them. They came to see and try to find a way round the problem,

They asked if Vera would mind if they dug a channel from the forestry to the river to take the water. Vera had a nine acre and twenty acre field that were rough grazing, so she said they could dig a channel down them. All was well for a while, then one day Vera had a young beast missing. The family walked and covered the field looking for what they thought was a sick animal pleading with their Lord to show them where it was as one animal seldom wanders off on its own; yet, it was not with the rest of the herd. Eventually after all hope was nearly exhausted it was spotted. No one had realised there was such a huge quantity of water going down the channel that the forestry had made. It had created a deep gulley. This heifer had fallen in. She was standing upright and not hurt, but no way could she get out as it was so narrow and deep—so deep, in fact, she could not be seen. She was recovered but Vera once again contacted the Forestry Commission and they made a channel elsewhere.

Vera went to count the beast early one morning and there were none in the field. Looking round the rest of the farm, she could not find them, so went round the field knowing if they had gone there must be a wall down or some escape route. Vera found the gate onto the forestry open. So getting Edward, they went up into the forest and searched and searched but could find nothing: no foot prints, no dung pats, no nothing. Knowing there were hundreds of acres of trees in the Cropton Forest did not ease the worry. As usual Vera prayed, and they eventually reached the watch tower which was built to reach up above the trees so a man could be sent up in tinder dry conditions to look out for any forest fires starting.

Vera knew the man on duty and asked if he had seen any animals but no he had not; they stood talking when Vera looked down and saw a the footprint of a beast. She was delighted and knew they couldn't be far. Searching the area, they found them contentedly standing in the trees. Being the mother, she was, although worn out by walking and searching, she arrived home not only with the beast but a huge bunch of beautiful heather for her daughter.

Vera had put some bales over from the dutch barn into the adjoining cattle shed to fill the feeding racks and bed the yard up. Rather than go round by the door, she climbed over the racks as she did every day but this day she slipped, and her foot caught. She was hanging upside down not knowing how to escape, realising Edward was not at home and Sylvia was working in the house and would never hear her shout, she just hung there. Eventually her Wellington started to slip, and she dropped heavily onto the floor of the shed. Vera came limping into the house. Edward was on an agricultural course. As soon as he came home, Sylvia had packed him his tea and told him to turn straight round as they had to take Mum to the doctor. Vera told the doctor what had happened, by this time her knee had swollen and was massive. He looked at it but did not examine It; he just wrote out a prescription.

She took it to the chemist, who said, "What's this for?"

So she showed him her knee. He looked aghast and said, "You should be in hospital."

The prescription was for a crepe bandage. No wonder Vera disliked doctors and would never go to them unless she was forced to do so. She was in agony and walked with two sticks for sixteen weeks.

Hartoft was about six miles from Goathland across country. Max Graham, who lived at Goathland, had a moor stray where his sheep grazed. Vera was in the field cleaning turnips when she saw some sheep which were not hers. She drove them off as sheep in a field of turnips do no good. They just take a nibble here and there at various turnips and then the bitten turnips go bad. Each day when she went to clean turnips the sheep were there, so she asked a neighbour if he knew whose initials "MG" were as that was what was on the sheep. He told her they would be Max Grahams, but she said, "Goathland is six miles away."

He explained that Max's moor stray was this side so would obviously be nearer. Vera phoned Max who rode over for them on his horse, but the sheep had got a taste of the turnips and were not going to give up that easily. They persisted in coming back. Max sent his son for them with a van so they could make them secure.

A short time later Vera went to the turnip field and here were two sheep back again. This happened several times. Each time Max got a phone call and came for them. The sheep got quite tame and would come close up to Vera, as she worked away at the turnips. She used to chatter to them, although a nuisance as far as the turnips were concerned Vera did love animals and had gotten quite fond of these two sheep.

Phoning Max one day he said, "Mrs. Stonehouse, you gather them up and take them to market. Keep half what they make towards damages and send me the other half."

That night a neighbour called in. Over supper Vera told him about the latest on the sheep and what Max had said about selling them and keeping half the money. Next time she went to clean the turnips the sheep had gone, but about a fortnight later Vera was working away when she heard: "Baa! Baa! Baa!"

And the two sheep came bounding over the wall.

"Hello, dears, where have you been?" asked Vera. As they came nearer, she saw the neighbours mark on them. She phoned Max and told him. He said Jim would come and get them. So he came with the van and Vera never saw any of Max's sheep again.

During one long hot summer in 1976 everything was tinder dry and the North York Moors caught fire. The blaze continued many days. The army was called in to help the fire fighters. Vera phoned the Forestry Commission to ask how near the fire was to her farm. They said everything possible was being done to keep it from the trees.

Vera and family were hay making at High Farm, the land Vera had bought at the opposite side of the dale to Head House. Most of the cattle were grazing at the far end of the farm at Head House. Vera's cousin, Albert Thornhill, who was Chief fire officer for Nottingham at that time, phoned; he had been following the fires progress on the news. He had contacts who had explained that the fire was coming in the direction of Hartoft and Head House.

He asked what lay between the farm and the fire. Vera's reply of "forestry" sent alarm bells ringing to a fire officer.

"What is in the fields between you and the trees?"

"Hay."

"Is it standing?"

"Yes."

"Then get it cut. The fire will not travel as fast down it if it is laid on the ground."

The Forestry Commission had said they would phone Vera if the fire reached the trees and Vera thought she would have enough time to evacuate after that phone call; however, Albert explained that the trees, being conifers, contained turpentine and when the flames hit them they would explode sending the flames through the forest with rapid speed and much faster than the fire was currently going through the heather.

Edward cut the hay immediately. Vera kept in touch with the forestry office and decided as soon as the fire hit the trees the family would drive the cattle to the other side of the river to the fields on the other side of the valley. Plans were made to put pets in the car and trailer. The sun was shining brightly causing no sense of alarm. Vera decided hay making must continue.

Vera stayed at Head House to be near the telephone. Much prayer was being sent up not only from the family but also from a lot of friends. Edward and Sylvia were trying to continue with the hay making at High Farm. Having to keep a look out every time the tractors turned at the end of the rows, Vera said she would hang a white sheet out of a bedroom window if the call to evacuate came. The brother and sister were filled with dismay when the valley suddenly filled with dense smoke. It was impossible to see anything. Leaving one of the tractors, they sped home as quickly as possible to find Vera on her knees.

"Get down quick, kids, and start praying. The forestry office say the wind has changed direction. The fire is almost at the trees. They will phone when it gets there. We will have to leave immediately. Only a change of wind direction can save the farm."

The realisation that because of the dense smoke they would never find the animals had never entered their heads until then.

Vera had a group of Christian friends who she had kept in touch with about the fire. She regularly phoned them asking to pray as different situations concerning how the fire developed. Now she rang them in desperation, explaining how the valley was filled with smoke and she could not see the animals to rescue them. She said to Edward and Sylvia to get on their knees. Vera sank on her knees and after placing all her faith and trust in her Lord, on rising to her feet, she looked out of the window saw the smoke vanish as quickly as it had arrived.

The different wind direction had been a boon to the fire fighters as they were able to work closer to the fire and won the battle. The same Lord who calmed the storm and wind on the sea for the disciples calmed the fire for Vera.

Chapter 15

HAVE I EVER TOLD YOU

VERA WAS RENOWNED FOR HER WARM HOSPITALITY: "Come on in. I'll put the kettle on," and with great speed the table was soon filled to capacity. As soon as the dear friends or relatives had their cup of tea and something to eat, Vera always started with her, "Have I ever told you?"

Her children loved her dearly, but before she started, they would say, "Yes, Mam, you have." And out would come some incident from her life. However hard she was working outside on the farm, entertaining was a great joy to Vera; no matter how tired, be it with hay making or wall building, cleaning out calf pens, if friends called—even if they were unexpected—the kettle was on, teapot soon filled, and food appeared. . . even at the busiest times.

Vera was a great cook. Her scones and dumplings were second to none. She would eat something different when out at a chapel supper or with at friends and say, "This is good," go home and make it. Then when cooked, would say, "This wants a bit more sugar or a bit less fat or this will be better if I add so and so," and she had a new recipe without the original recipe.

Fastening the hens up one night, it was nearly dark, when she heard voices.

"Don't tell any secrets because I'm here," she said.

Two young men appeared. "Can you tell us where we are? We have been walking on the moors and got lost in the forest. Do you know where we can get beds for the night?"

"Come on in and have a cup of tea. We will try and find you somewhere."

Supper was prepared and eaten, and the pair thoroughly warmed through by the fire. Then the phone calls proceeded to find them beds for the night. The only vacancies were at a hotel in Rosedale Abbey. Vera told Edward to take them in the car as it was a distance of five miles. It was dark and they were tired. They said they would be all right, but Vera was having none of it. Then she noticed they were trying to leave some money, but Vera was as quick as they were and told them to put it in their pockets. This was the beginning of many years friendship. Jeremy Boatright she never heard of again, but Patrick Fendle, when he arrived back in London, sent many gifts and cards, letters, and tea towels from places he visited over the years. His writing was beautiful Copper Plate. The postman always commented on it when he handed the letters over.

Patrick had friends in Barnard Castle. He used to fly from London to see them and they would bring him down to the farm. Even when he had a kidney transplant in later years, he never forgot Vera and family. Five years after his transplant, the communications stopped. A letter was sent from Hartoft to his address in London asking if he was all right. A reply was received from the new tenant of the flat to say that she did not know much about him but did know that he had passed away suddenly and his only known relative was his step-mother.

Vera saw and proved the love and goodness and faithfulness of the Lord many times a day. She knew she was a sinner saved by grace; knowing whatever bitter words were spoken to her—and there were many—with her being a woman in business, that she could take everything to her Lord in prayer, the One who poured a soothing healing balm on all her troubles and worries.

When she purchased the land at High Farm on the other side of the valley to Head House, Vera purchased two lorries, a flatbed to lead the straw, and a tipper to lead the corn. This took away the problem of tractors and trailers jack-knifing, crossing the steep valley with heavy loads behind them. One brilliant sunny day during harvest, Vera, Edward, and Sylvia were crossing the fields with a lorry load of straw bales at High Farm when a large number of vehicles came along and parked on the grass verges by the side of the field gate.

Vera said, "I don't believe it. It is the shooting syndicate." At that time the syndicate was not made up of titled gentry, but workers and managing directors. As the men were getting their guns out of the vehicles and putting on their Wellingtons, their women folk who must have been attracted by the glorious weather, were coming in through the field gateway into the field as Vera's lorry approached to go out onto the road.

Vera raised her hand in a friendly wave as she passed them but the so called "ladies" tossed their heads in the air and turned the other way. Vera said, "That is the last time they have my shooting." And it was.

Vera loved and trusted her Lord and Saviour; this was known to all who knew her. No one was ever left in any doubt. The blessings He mercifully bestowed upon her were many—far too numerous to name them all.

Vera laboured hard and toiled hours long in difficult situations. For many years the skin on her fingers and feet cracked and were very painful, yet there was always her Lord watching lovingly over her.

Vera was resourceful and had a wonderful ability to make something out of nothing. She would go around at lambing time and find any spars that had broken out of field gates and any old zinc or corrugated iron sheets and nailed them together making hurdles to make lambing pens for the sheep. After lambing the hurdles would be knocked apart and the field gates mended. Often at a farm sale—Vera loved farm sales—she would look longingly at a pile of timber going for a pound or two, but she did not have a trailer at that time and to pay for the haulage was out of the question.

Many hill farmers such as Vera had a struggle both financially and with the workload could have done with a retired or part-time workman a few hours now and then, but even then, many did not like hard work. Something for nothing, yes, but work, no.

Vera wanted to reclaim some rough land. It had quite a lot of trees on it, so Vera said to the local cottagers that they could have any of the trees for firewood so long as they cleared the thin branches or "brash", as it was known. She said it was okay to fire it so long as they got rid of it at the same time as they cleared the trees. She kept seeing the loads of wood going to the various cottages; even one farmer was coming for it. She thought they were doing very well to be clearing it so quickly as she had not seen any smoke. She thought they must be taking the small branches for kindling to start the fires at home. As Vera was wanting to get a contractor in to plough the field, she thought she would have a walk over and see how the trees were going. She got the shock of her life when she saw heaps and heaps of the branches. Trees had been felled and the trunks and good firewood had been taken, but all the thin branches left.

Vera was really annoyed and went to the cottages and told the occupants there were no more trees to be had and told them in no uncertain terms why. It was amazing that not one recipient of the timber had made an effort to burn the branches.

Vera was always blessed with an abundant supply of turnips. One year they were hit by the pest, "black fly". She phoned agricultural contractors to try to get someone with a sprayer, but the black fly was prevalent that year and no one was available. Realising she was going to lose all her crops, she told Edward to fill all the milk churns with water and take them to the six acre field, Then Vera, Edward, and Sylvia armed with a bucket and a small empty can tinned vegetables had come in, filled the buckets with water, put a measure of Jeyes Fluid into the buckets, and watered all the turnips in the field. It was a back breaking and painstaking job, but the crops was saved.

One year there was an abundant supply of turnips. Vera told a local couple from the chapel that they could have a load or two for their cows if they would clean them and fetch them. They were delighted and soon came for a load or two. Vera could not believe her eyes when she went to the field to clean turnips, instead of cleaning two rows and throwing them to the right, then the next two rows and throwing them to the left, then cleaning the next four rows in the same manner so the tractor and trailer could pull between them to be loaded, they had gone all over the field pulling all the big turnips out and leaving the smaller ones so Vera had to tell them there was no more turnips available.

Vera's daughter had wanted a little dog from a very young age. When they lived at Sawdon, it was always top of the list at Christmas, but her father said a definite no. While Vera was shopping in Falsgrave at Scarborough, Eddie took the bairns to see the monkey, which at that time used to be in the animal sanctuary window, but Sylvia never saw the monkey. In the other window were two cute little mongrel pups, a black one and a white one. Vera came out of a shop to see Eddie waving frantically for her to come.

"I've put my foot in it now," he said. "Bairn saw them pups and to put her off I went in and asked the price thinking I could tell her they were too dear, but they are free to a good home."

That was how dear little Boo, who became Booie was a much loved pet for seven years. It was at Head House one snowy winter's night that she was ill. Vera phoned the farm's vet, Peter Fernie, to see if she could take Booie down to the surgery. He said no, just give her an aspirin. Sylvia stayed up with a very sick little dog overnight. A heavy fall of snow came, and the family had to dig tracks to get the car across the dale next morning to get to Pickering. The vet said there was nothing that could be done. He thought it was inflammation of the womb. The family rushed to the vet at the animal sanctuary at Scarborough, who also said nothing could be done and little Boo died that night in loving arms, aged seven years, never to be forgotten by the family.

About a fortnight later, the vet, Peter Fernie, was shooting with the syndicate that had the shooting on the farm at that time. He came to the farmhouse door with a black Labrador. Vera remarked about the dog.

"This dog is worth a fortune," he said.

"Yes, and I'd have given everything I have to have saved the life of ours." replied Vera.

At Wombleton Aerodrome there was a collective implement sale from time to time where farmers would take implements and machinery they no longer needed, to be sold by auction. It was here that Vera was interested in a binder as hers was getting past its best. It was before combine harvesters were available. Bidding for it, she suddenly stopped, whispered to her family that she was sure the auctioneer didn't have another bidder but was "running it" himself.

"Come on! Just another bid; it isn't the price of a dozen eggs."

Vera refused. He tried and tried to persuade her to bid again but she firmly said no. Whether he was "running it" by bidding himself she never found out, but that binder stopped on the aerodrome for weeks.

At the Driffield implement sale Vera purchased a plough and she had a word with John Pennock who did the farm haulage. He said he would deliver it. He nearly had a load of machinery for other farmers but said he could fit it in.

On the Sunday morning, the family heard a lorry coming up the hill to the farm. With the road being so steep, any vehicles approaching the farm could be heard long before they arrived. When it came in sight it was John. Vera went out and reprimanded John, who was a friend of the family having gone to school at the same time as Vera's two children—they regarded him and his work highly.

"John, how can you do this to me? You know we don't work on the Lord's day and do nothing more than make the animals comfortable. This plough could have been brought anytime," said Vera.

"Sorry, Mrs. Stonehouse, but I had nearly got loaded when you mentioned the plough so it went on last and I can't get anything off till I get rid of it; but it won't happen again," replied John.

Winter arrived and with it a covering of snow. A cow had gone down in the cow house which made it difficult getting the cows in and out for milking. The vet was not hopeful of her recovery and after a few days she died lying on her side with her legs outstretched and stomach "blown up" on the Lord's day morning. It was impossible to get the cows past her into the cow house to milk them.

John had brought a load to the farm on the Saturday and had broken down in the valley bottom. Not actually on the farm, so on the Lord's day morning when his brother, David, was off work, he got him to come and give the lorry a tow home. Knowing he had a winch Edward went down to ask him if he would winch the cow out of the way. He said he was quite willing to do this. On reaching the farmyard, he met a very worried Vera. A dead cow stuck in the doorway and unable to get a herd of cows into the cow house for milking.

David said, "Mrs. Stonehouse, we would gladly have winched your cow out of the way, but we can't, you see. Its Sunday and you told us not to do anything on your farm on the Lord's day." Talk about getting your own back; of course, David did move the cow as Vera said it was a case of getting the donkey out of the pit as the Bible says.

Vera so loved attending the furniture sales. They were held at the owners' property then, not so much at salerooms. At Hackness, she had a look around before the sale since it was held at the brother and sister's home. They were retired farmers, so a lot of the small items were in boxes and stacked under tables. It was up to viewers to look through them and see what there was.

Vera's daughter came up to her and said she had found a lovely velvet and silver pin cushion in a box. She was collecting Victorian pin cushions at that time and asked her mum to buy her the box, if at all possible. Vera kept her eye on the box. There was a retaining wall at the back of the house keeping the soil away from the house walls; between this and the house the auctioneers had placed trestle tables with all manner of crockery and glassware. Vera and her friend, Doris Nesfield, decided to stand on the embankment at the back of the wall so they could see over the tables and have a good view when the auctioneer came to sell. Framed pictures were stacked at the bottom of the retaining wall, so Vera's little party had a good view from their vantage point. Vera was looking down at the people going through the pictures. A man wearing a leather jacket with large pockets was bent down looking through the pictures. As he bent his pocket opened.

Vera let out a yell, pointing to the man. She screamed, "That man has that pincushion you wanted in his pocket!"

Sure enough, there it was for all to see. He jumped up and hurried from the area.

"Do you know him?" Vera asked those around her.

"Yes," someone replied. "He is our doctor!" The sale had not even started.

Vera was very reluctant to buy anything for anyone else at the sales after her sister, Rosie, put her in to buy a tin bath for her. Bathrooms had not been thought of. Vera bought it but after the sale it had taken legs, or rather someone on legs had taken it. Vera had already paid for it so was greatly distressed. Every penny counted in Vera's meagre resources, but she was even more distressed when her sister refused to pay for it, despite being on a farm with a fat milk cheque coming in.

"I have not got my bath," she said.

"Neither have I," said Vera.

Vera's baler was on its last legs and there was one exactly like it at a farm sale at Lockton, so off she went with her family. When she arrived, she thought, "oh no!" There was her brother and two sisters looking around the baler. They told her in no uncertain terms they had come for the baler and she must not "run them", in other words, bid against them. Vera's son was bitterly disappointed as by this time he was doing most of the repairs and with this one, which was in very good condition, he could use the old one for spares.

"How much will you be going to for it," asked Vera.

"Oh, we shall buy it. We need it," Rosie said.

Vera stood back when the auctioneer came to the baler and was dumb-founded when she saw they were not bidding. She made her way through the crowd but by the time she got to the auctioneer he had knocked it down to someone else.

"You never bid at all!" She yelled at her sister

"No. I should think not. It was too dear."

Vera was heartbroken.

There was a furniture sale at Kirkbymoorside at the home of an elderly lady. There were tables of interesting bric a bac. Vera had got a good vantage point to see over the tables with their varied array of treasures and keepsakes. A youth stood near the table, picking several items up and looking at them, in particular a beautiful solid silver hunter pocket watch. Every time he picked it up, he put it down nearer to him. Vera drew several people's attention to this, when all of a sudden, he picked it up and shot out through the crowd. Several grabbed hold of him and made him turf it out.

"It's mine," he said. "It has my name inscribed in it." He was not the sort of person to have a silver hunter watch inscribed with his name neither was the age he would have needed to be. "The lady whose sale it was had passed away," Vera told Peter Woodall, the auctioneer, and staff kept their eye on him at other sales. They soon discovered he had an accomplice who stood at the back of the crowd with an air of not being interested in proceedings but with a bag on his back.

It was at this sale that once again with being a lot of bric a bac and the lady being deceased, a lot of things were in big boxes and the buyers had to sort through to see what there was in them. Sylvia pointed out to Vera a box and asked her to buy it if she could, and also said she was interested in a bundle of walking sticks. There were three gun cleaners in the bundle and obviously someone had noticed and paid a lot of money for them but that was not a problem as Vera had one at home. When the box came up, Vera bought it for five shillings.

"Well," Sylvia said, "he has got the gun cleaners, but we have got all the brass nozzles for the ends." And sure enough, when the family got home, they fitted their gun cleaner which up until then they had no nozzles.

At a sale at the beautiful village of Levisham, the house holder had laid the small household items on tables on the green in front of the house. Peter Woodall was not the auctioneer at this sale. Vera saw a small brass crook like one she had at home. While waiting for the sale to start she was looking around. The auctioneer stood talking to a group of farmers with the crook in his hand. When the group of farmers departed, he went to his car and put the crook in. Vera, although she did not know the householder, told her what happened; the lady went to the auctioneer and told him what had been seen. So he had to go and get it out of the car.

Vera bought Sylvia a pony. She had not had one before. She obtained it from Harry Atkinson whom she had known for years as they both came from the Driffield area. He was an expert on horses. After some weeks, Sylvia was on the horse when it reared into the air. Another day she went to put the bridle on and the pony charged at her with its mouth open, baring its teeth. Sometimes it was all right then vicious. It was explained to the belief that Sylvia was nervous of it. Then Vera, who was brought up with horses, was alarmed at its behavior. She contacted Harry and explained, although her daughter was an adult, this was her first pony. Its behaviour was alarming. He immediately said he would change it or give her the money back. He had been told it was a child's pony but had no way of proving this. He sent his men for it straight away. They put it in a field with some more horses. There was a fight and they could not separate them. They had to take the humane killer and shoot Chester (as the child's pony had been named). It was obvious that the horse had never been castrated properly and therefore would fight with the other stallion in the field.

However, soon after Vera and family were in Harry's yard on another matter, they saw with the other horses the dearest tiny grey pony only waist high. Vera bought the lovely little girl. She was named Lavinia but always called Vinny. She was six years old; but, was with Vera and family and brought great pleasure for another thirty years travelling with them when they moved to the Scottish borders and later when they lived in Caithness.

Vera was many years without a pet dog in the house after little Boo's death as the loss had made her daughter very ill. Then it was decided it was time for another little life to be rescued and Bambi came as a pup from a house in Scarborough. Bambi was black and white a terrier cross and was much loved and gave much love. Central heating was virtually unheard of and the bedrooms were very cold, so Vera used to kneel and say her prayers in the kitchen before she went to bed. As soon as Vera knelt, Bambi would poke her with her nose and Vera would move to the side. Then Bambi would jump into the chair Vera was kneeling at and sit there until prayers were finished. Vera said it was as if he knew that she was communing with her Lord and wanted to be included.

Wherever the family went when they reached the village of Wrelton where the road turned off for Cropton then Hartoft, Vera always sent a telepathic message, "Put the kettle on Bambi."

No matter where she had been Vera always loved a cup of tea as soon as she arrived home. Dear Bambi also lived with the family for many years and moved to Scotland like Vinnie with them.

The sheep were always brought into the farmyard if there was snow forecast. With being on the North Yorkshire moors, the snow falls where heavy and often lasted for six weeks. The sheep, one winter, had been brought into the yard; it had been quite a lot of snow and was deep.

Vera always slept in a back bedroom with her window opened a little so she could hear the animals should there be any problems. On this particular night she woke the family saying she thought the sheep had got out of the yard. Vera and Sylvia slipped on their wellies and a coat and ran outside. A gate had blown down and the sheep had gone out but had found a load of turnips which had been emptied at the end of the dutch barn. Vera got to one end and Sylvia ran to the other, so they had the sheep contained until Edward came to help get them back into the yard.

They waited and waited but no Edward appeared. They knew as soon as one of them moved the sheep would be tired of the turnips and be off. Freezing in the bitter cold, it was decided Sylvia should go and find him. On arriving back at the house, she found him tucked up in bed. He had drifted off to sleep again. However, as soon as Sylvia left her end, the sheep had rushed back to their field. It was too dark to find them, so it was abandoned until daylight. Thankfully there was no more snow that night.

The family had gone to bed one night when there was the loudest bang. They slept with their doors ajar.

"What was that?" everyone said together.

Vera got up and took a stick and went the length of the house, upstairs to the bathroom, examining it and the two spare bedrooms. She looked up into the loft.

"All seems all right up here. Listen for me. I'm going downstairs," she said. Slowly and methodically she went around the two rooms, kitchen, pantry, back kitchen. Having found nothing, she came back upstairs to bed.

"All's clear kids."

Silence!

"All's clear." Silence!

Both had gone back to sleep! Vera said the next morning, "What if there had been anyone in? A lot of good you two would have been."

George Watson from Northdale was a good friend of the family. He went to school with Sylvia and the families met at chapels at Sunday school and chapel anniversaries in the early days at Hartoft. Later Edward and George were regular visitors to each other's farms. Mrs. Watson was a very sweet, gentle, and gracious lady; not like you would expect on a hill farm, she was much loved by the family. Her husband was a tall kindly man who thought the world of his wife and his family. Their daughter married and went to live at East Ayton. Vera loved a ride up to Northdale to visit them.

The Atkinson Family at Lastingham were also great friends and visits to each other's chapels were enjoyed, especially the Christmas singing each year on Christmas night around Lastingham. Vera had a great affection for young Edward and for many years, even when miles away, would phone to see how he was keeping and how the farm was doing. She was greatly saddened by his early passing.

One year while carol singing after several glasses of ginger wine kindly given, Vera felt the need of a toilet. "Oh," Mrs. Atkinson said, "just pop down that little lane. No one will go down there at this time of night." So down Vera went down when all of a sudden, a young lady with the party with a powerful torch shone it up and down the lane shouting, "Where has Mrs. Stonhouse gone? Where is Mrs. Stonhouse?"

Mrs. Atkinson kept coops of little ducks and chickens on the grass at the side of the road outside their farmhouse in the village; these were quite an attraction to visitors in summer and were often photographed.

Brenda and Hector Johnson, who farmed at Chopgate, near Stokesley, and were Methodists, were very dear to Vera. She loved to talk to Hector about farming and chapel. Same as Vera, they had a lot of snow in winter, but they usually managed to travel to each other's farms and had some lovely evenings, especially at Christmas. One visit which Vera remembered fondly, was when arriving at their farm, Gillian, their daughter—six years old at the time— came to the door, "Come in. Mum will be downstairs in a minute."

On taking Vera and family through to the living room said, "Just a moment. I will warm these for you." She picked up two cushions from out of an armchair and took them to the fireside and held them in front of the fire— wonderful act of kindness never forgotten. Vera adored Gillian's brother,

David, and right up to the end of her life, her face lit up and was wreathed in smiles when David entered the room. As a young lad he always went to her and this made her feel so special.

Vera had one special reading in the Yorkshire dialect which she learnt and said when the family took Sacred Concerts when she was young and still said up to her 100th birthday.

There was yance a moose an it warn't a very big moose,
It was only a middlenish size sort o moose.
An it hed get its hool at side of a greet vat iv a brewery,
Ya day lartle moose chanced ti fall intid drink, an sed tiv his sen
What sall ah deeh noo, ah'll lettie swim roond an roond till aahs droonded.
Just then cat chanced ti come along,
"What's thou doing id drink?" cat asks.
"What will thou gimme if ah gets thou oot,
Why sez lartle moose thou sall have me."
So cat hings her sen our'd side od vat
An lartle moose clims up cat back
An lept right frav top od cat back intiv its hool
An starts ti laugh at cat
"Why" sez cat, "I thowt thou sed I should hey thou."
"I," sez moose, "fooks aal say owt when they're in drink."

Vera loved clean jokes and riddles; her favourite which she asked regularly again right up till she was a hundred years old.

A visitor went to Egypt and was being shown round a museum. The guide showed him some large earthenware jars, and said, "Now in those jars are the bones of Pharaoh's lean kine." The visitor laughed. Why did he laugh?

Vera saw many great preachers and Bible scholars stumble. "Oh, the lean ate the fat!" "No, the fat ate the lean," and so on. The answer of course was, "It was a Dream!"

Part Two

Chapter 16

BATTLE SHIPS AND AEROPLANES

VERA NEEDED ANOTHER CAR; although she never drove or did anything mechanical herself. She loved vehicles and had a great love for cars. Deciding to go to a car auction—loving auction sales of any kind—was an automatic decision. Living across the dale with its steep hills, it had to be a powerful car., Edward took Vera and Sylvia to Bawtry. Having had a look around, she was quite disappointed there was not anything suitable for pulling a trailer. Vera was feeling a little dejected. It had been a long journey and to be away from a busy working farm required a lot of preparation. Walking away from the main building, she was taken very much by surprise when a huge brilliant red and white gull winged American Chevrolet Impala was driven from off the road and straight into the queue going through to the sale room.

"That must be for sale!" she cried and made haste for the front of the rostrum. This was a beautiful car but totally unsuitable for pulling a trailer or travelling on narrow country roads; although it had one important factor—Vera loved it on sight. By the time she arrived at the rostrum, the car was there. She had never seen or heard the engine running or inspected it in any way until then.

The auctioneer said this car had belonged to Pinewood Film Studio's at one time and had appeared in a film with Peter Sellers. Vera, at that moment, was not interested in Peter Sellers; she just loved this car. She bid and bought it.

On arriving at the office to pay for it she was asked for her Bankers Order. Poor Vera did not know the ins and outs of car auctions, did not know that you could not just walk in, and pay with a cheque. After all, that's all she had done all her life at auctions. The clerk was very nice but said, "You are not known to us."

Here Vera's Christian walk with her beloved Lord came to the forefront. The staff decided her honest face and manner were sufficient and accepted her cheque. After telephoning the National Farmers Union to get the car insured, Vera was able to take her car home. Vera, who never gave much thought to worldly things, really loved that car. It was never sold until it was scrap and then very reluctantly, probably its low number of XLU 11 has still survived. The car was still, at the time of writing, some forty years on remembered at the little country chapels where Vera loved to go to the chapel and Sunday school anniversaries and when various gospel choirs were visiting. Saturday evenings, for years were taken up washing and polishing it to travel to the Breaking of Bread at the Thirsk and later Driffield Brethren Assemblies.

Later Vera purchased a Jaguar Mark Mk10. She had previously had a Jaguar Mk 5 convertible, which she never used, and it was sold; only to find out in later years there were not many made, and it was worth quite a lot of money. She had a Mk 7m and an Mk 7 that had had a Perkins diesel engine fitted and an Mk 9 which she gave her daughter for her twenty first birthday. The Mk10 and the Chevrolet were at Head House together and parked in the yard when Vera's brothers and sisters came to visit. Rosie, the youngest sister, got out of the car and said, "You are not satisfied with a car. Now you have got a battleship and an aeroplane."

The Jaguar MK10 also had the low registration number of GVN 7, though this was not of much financial significance in those days.

Vera had made many improvements to Head House Farm: making a good road, having a dutch barn, yard to house cattle, and an implement shed, crop store, and calf pens.

The farm had no hedges; it was all stone walls. These Vera kept in good repair, rebuilding them all herself as they fell down, or as stones came or were knocked off. Vera even built stone terraces in the garden. These were filled with manure and soil. Vera asked her good friend, Dick Turner from Bridlington, if he would fill them with roses. This he did with seventy-two rose bushes, different named varieties and colours.

Whatever house or farm Vera moved to, one of her first moves was to start making a lovely garden. In some cases, this meant sawing trees down and digging roots out by hand. Vera and Eddie were never any good with machinery; thankfully their son was.

In the early days at Hartoft, Vera walked most Sundays in the afternoon to the little chapel and for some time played the organ. After a while she suggested to Herbert Allanson, who was the chapel steward, that it would be nice to have an anniversary service; he had a large family and there were quite a few children in the area. She attained this with a resounding success.

Walking was something Vera and family had to get used to. As mentioned, Vera could not drive on going to Hartoft and Edward was only fifteen. The family would have a long walk to a farm near Rosedale to friends Fred and Sarah Hall at Christmas, sometimes through deep snow.

It made a huge difference when Edward passed his driving test. The family would go to the Driffield Gospel Hall on the Lord's day morning. Vera's dear friends, Milly and George Binks, would provide dinner. If for any reason the morning meeting could not be attended, then they would go for evening service, where once again they would be treated after the service to a supper at George and Milly's with any other visitors and what a spread that was.

In winter on the North York moors, the farm was easily cut off by snow for six weeks at a time. So on the mention of snow in the weather forecast, Edward would take the car across the valley, so the family could walk across and not have to dig the valley out. Vera was never afraid of snow and every autumn would stockpile flour, sugar, dried yeast, breakfast cereals. The family never went hungry.

Edward and Sylvia were never surprised there would be deep snow. All the animals would be fed, and Vera would say, "Let's go to Hackness to see her brothers and sisters."

They had to walk across the dale to where Edward had left the car. When the snow was forecast, they had many exciting journeys travelling there and back, but it never bothered Vera if they got stuck. "We'll just get on and dig out."

Vera had a caravan on the farm for friends to come and stay. One of the families were Bob and Nina Cargill from St Monans in Fife. Later Bert, their son, and his family—after visiting many times—mentioned it was their Christian Conference and Vera decided it would be nice to attend.

The family rose early, milked the cows, fed the cattle, and away they went. Newcastle was reached, and they saw a signpost informing them Edinburgh was still over a hundred miles away, and St Monans was quite a bit further than that. They arrived in time for the afternoon conference, stayed for the evening, and had supper. The advice given for the return journey was at this time of night go straight through Edinburgh. There was not much traffic about, keep the castle on your left hand side, you can't go wrong. Who were they kidding! There were very few signs and after a very long time seeming to go around and around, thinking they were leaving the city, Vera said, "The castle is still on my left hand side!"

They did arrive home in the early hours and then had the cows to milk and animals to feed. Vera was calm throughout and never batted an eyelid; she was just delighted to have been to the conference.

Vera was determined to have some evangelical meetings in the area and booked the scout hall in Helmsley. Once a month on a Saturday night, Basil Lauriston from Redcar, whose Aunt Vera had known from the gospel meetings in Driffield, found some very able speakers. Some lovely evenings were had.

A very able hostess, Vera loved cooking and entertaining. She had a large lawn sown in the garden. A party was planned, and Edward went to cut the lawn, but the mower failed to start. Panic set in. The lawn desperately needed cutting but the mower would not go. Vera, determined her party was going ahead, took out the kitchen scissors and cut the lawn. How she got it finished no one ever knew, but she did, and the party went ahead with no one the wiser.

One chapel Vera loved to visit was Farndale. Arthur Carter and the Aconleys always made her so welcome. It was here she first heard the Orton Male Voice Praise Choir. She loved Orton Male Voice Choirs ever after. Sometime after coming to Farndale, the Orton MVP Choir attended Potterhill Chapel at Pickering.

The chapel was large and was packed out. Just before the choir was due to come in to sing, a deathly quiet crept over the congregation when someone must have asked a local boddy a very personal question and in loud strident tones she volleyed forth, "Oh nah! nah! I'se nut tellin tha, if ah tells thee thou'll knaw as much as me an its tha job ti find oot."

Chapter 17

TIME TO MOVE ON

IT WAS APRIL 1979 WHEN VERA MOVED FROM HARTOFT. She had bought three farms at Hartoft: firstly, Head House, then Birch House—although all the time Vera owned Birch House it was tenanted by Francis Boddy. She also purchased the land of High Farm to enable her to be self-sufficient. All the hay and turnips Vera required could be grown at Head House. The land at High Farm was mostly arable. She could grow all the corn she needed for feed and straw for bedding for the stock. As she approached seventy years of age Vera began to slow down a little—not noticeable to anyone else—but she felt it within herself and her son, Edward, was not well.

Vera realized it was time to downsize. Several properties were viewed and had drawbacks. Vera's idea was to purchase a property with a large house and a paddock or two, so that a few of the farm favourites could be taken and some of the farm tools, but also a large house so Vera and Sylvia could take paying guests—either as Bed and Breakfast or on a weekly basis. Hard work perhaps, but not as hard as lifting bales of hay and straw, bags of barley for the cattle, and heavy stones for the building of the dry stone walls. Vera viewed many properties.

She always went to look at the outside of the properties first so that if the surroundings or area were not to her liking, she had not troubled the estate agents or owners.

Vera was interested in a property at Huddersfield. The family went to view it. It was a lovely large house in beautiful surroundings; it had paddocks, a large vegetable garden, a greenhouse, and flower garden—everything Vera wanted. It was in a quiet situation not much traffic. All of a sudden cars and vehicles started coming past; nose to tail on and on they came.

A lady was walking past with a small dog, Vera said to her, "What has happened? It was so quiet and then all this traffic."

"Oh, this happens when the shifts change. The David Brown Tractor Works are just round the corner. When they do it is impossible to get out of our drives."

Viewing many properties and giving each much prayer and consideration—Vera never did anything in private or business life without taking it to her Lord in prayer– she did not feel led to any of them.

A floor had been washed at Head House and newspapers put down for dirty wellingtons to walk on. The photo of a large house caught Vera's eye. She bent down and read the article accompanying it.

She said, "How does a house with eleven bedrooms, plus a cottage and a large range of buildings and two fields sound?"

This was Monday and offers had to be in on the Friday. It was a former shooting lodge in the Scottish Borders. Vera got permission to view and next day the family made their way north. They all loved the place, so Vera put in an offer which was eventually accepted.

As soon as Newlands was purchased Vera had to go to Scotland for the keys to be handed over. The family put five large stone troughs they were taking with them into their Richardson trailer. They realised they could be left in Scotland without much fear of being stolen, as they were so heavy. Soon into the journey they realized this was a mistake. Although it was a powerful, their Ford Falcon was not powerful enough for hauling five stone troughs. The journey took many hours. They eventually arrived at Newlands which was nearly 200 miles—only to find the solicitor never arrived with the keys as had been arranged. This being 1979 there were no mobile phones. They drove down to the Village of Newcastleton and phoned the solicitor. He said he was unable to leave the office and the keys would have to be collected.

The trailer and troughs were left at Newlands and the weary family had to travel another eighty miles to Dumfries and back to collect the keys. Not even a cup of tea was offered. Flasks had not been packed as it was thought as soon as the solicitor handed over the keys, Vera could soon make a cuppa since they had an electric kettle with them.

Arriving back at Newlands with the keys it was discovered the electricity had been disconnected, by now it was very late and there were dogs and the other animals at Hartoft needing feeding. It was a very long day without food and drink.

Part of the land Head House was retained and a shed. It was arranged with the farmers moving into the farm to allow financial relief if they would look after some of the cows, until it was seen if Edward recovered and wanted to go farming again. Sadly, they went off their part of the bargain. The wife phoned one day to say the bull was out again. They could not keep him in, and he was wandering all over the dale.

Vera phoned Cundalls and arranged to take the bull to Malton Market. When they arrived at Head House, all the neighbours said the bull was fine, no problem at all. The only time he got out was when a Francis Boddy, who farmed Birch House, had some heifers in the next field requiring a bull. It was not the bull's fault, Vera realized. They had got tired of tending her cattle. Because there would just be more trouble, more farmland was purchased at Newcastleton and some of the cows were moved north.

The property in Scotland was being sold by the Buccleaugh Estates; it required much attention. Vera quickly got the large walled garden into production, growing her own potatoes and vegetables, fruit and flowers. She was sixty nine years old but dug it all herself, kept it weeded and planted.

The rooms were large and very tall which gave Vera a problem on how to decorate the ceilings. She had always with a little help from Edward and

Sylvia decorated her own homes. Vera never liked painting but putting wall-paper on was never a problem. It was only if someone was helping. It did not take long for Vera to come up with an idea to cope with the high ceilings on her own. She bought extra wallpaper the colour she was doing the rooms and rolls of white wallpaper. She would then cut the wallpaper into squares the size of the width of the rolls, paste them, and put them up alternately. This size she could manage, even at the top of the steps. Everyone visiting the house remarked on the lovely ceilings. The idea was very effective. The doors were large and paneled so Vera had the idea of papering the panels with the same wallpaper as the room then there was not so much for Sylvia to paint.

Edward and Sylvia were travelling to Yorkshire twice a week to fetch fur-niture, tools, and hay from the farm. Papering and scrubbing out rooms kept Vera entertained while they were away, as it was a long slow journey in the lorry. They set off early in the morning and came back the same day.

Vera loved clocks and organs. She had a huge organ which had at one time had a handle to pump to blow air into it to make it play. It had a motor put on at a later date to save the poor human having all the hard work. This motor was ridiculously heavy, but it had to be moved to Scotland. Vera also had an Aeolian Organ which had 72 rolls. It was purchased when friends bought Sevenford House in Rosedale. The friends were looking for a large house to retire to and Vera knew this one was for sale. She told them about it and that she had been to see if it was suitable for her brothers and sisters to retire to. She said there was just one thing if they bought it, she would love the organ. They bought the place, then it was found the organ would not come out through the door. The furniture removers said it had gone in through one of the large windows, but the friends said that no way were they taking a window out. So, Edward partly dismantled and rebuilt it. The organ was a marvelous piece of engineering, similar to a pianola and Vera loved it. One just had to put a roll in and pedal. One of the rolls Vera liked was based on Scottish melodies. The rolls always had written on them which organ stops to pull out. When this was done and the roll put in and the pedaling commenced, it just sounded like bagpipes. These huge organs had to be dismantled to move to Scotland. It was many weeks that Vera was left on her own to decorate the place.

On the way home late at night with one load, the lorry broke down in Keilder Forest. Edward found out it was a fuel problem but after some time of trying to mend it, was able to bypass it with a rubber pipe stuck in a drum of diesel. Sylvia had to nurse this all the way home, to make sure the pipe did not come out. As previously said, there were no mobile phones in 1979 and the phone was not connected at Newlands. When they reached home the ever practical Vera said, "I thought you must have had an accident, but I had decided if you had been killed, I was going to part with the main house and live in the cottage."

Chapter 18

HEALTH PROBLEMS

WHILE HELPING TO EMPTY THE LORRY after one of these journeys back to the farm, Vera complained of severe abdominal pain. Vera was not one for going to the doctor. Her grandmother was well known for her herbal cures. Vera was more often heard to say, "You will have to pray for me, bairns, I have some pain."

She had far more faith in her Lord than in any doctor. In this instance Vera had been helping to lift lorry and car engines off the lorry. No one doubted she easily could be in some pain. After a day or two the pain was not getting any easier and she was persuaded to go to the doctor, He was most amused after having told Vera to undress at the back of a screen. Ready to examine her, he went around the screen and found her on the couch with a blanket wrapped round her and her large brimmed felt hat still on. Vera was always very smart and usually wore a hat and gloves and had a large selection of them; her favourites were kid gloves in winter and pretty lacy crochet ones in summer. She loved her jewellery—never earrings but always beads and a brooch and usually a bracelet. She had her favourites and was only known to wear one silver one for years. When her husband had been helping to empty a house, he brought home a curtain pole, with a selection of large brass curtain rings on it.

"Is this any use?" he asked.

Looking at it, Vera said, "That is." And selecting one of them she exclaimed, "That's no curtain ring." She slid it off the pole, cleaned it up, and found a fastener on it. She now had a lovely silver bracelet which was the only bracelet she wore for years. She did eventually find another old one which she cleaned up. This one was brass, and she only ever wore one of these two bracelets.

There was a stall at the bottom end of Scarborough Market Hall. A Mr. Todd had it; he had all sorts of bric-a-bac, and Vera loved to rummage through the boxes looking for pretty beads and brooches. Eddie loved a rummage on the stall too for small tools and books.

In the Market Hall, Neville Coates had a butchers stall and good meat was to be had there. It was frequented by many farmers' wives. Vera would go there to buy a breast of mutton and get her dripping. Another butcher of renown was Arthur Johnson up Aberdeen Walk. He was usually known as "Arthur Willie". He sold very good pork pies and most farmers had to have a trip up to Arthur Willies for pork pies when in the town.

Dr. Marshall at Newcastleton, who examined Vera, thought her pain was coming from her gallbladder. He sent her to Carlisle Infirmary where they discovered it was not gall stones but a blocked gallbladder. She was hospitalised for the first time in her life. At first, she accepted the situation, although she had a great fear of hospitals. She was heavily drugged and was virtually unconscious for two or three days. Edward and Sylvia could not rouse her. They went to visit in the afternoon, had a look round Carlisle between visiting times, then went for the evening visit before going home to Newcastleton.

Edward said there was no need to stay as she did not know them, but Sylvia insisted. Friends and relatives were praying for Vera and when Edward and Sylvia got home the phone never stopped ringing. They did eventually manage between calls to milk the house cow and walk the dogs and tend the sheep. They arrived one afternoon to find Vera in a distressed state. The nurses had been trying to give her tablets and she had been refusing them, as she had only been on drip with nil by mouth, she had not been passing anything. The doctors decided to put a pessary up the rectum that was a non-runner from the start.

The next day the family got a phone call from the hospital, "Will you come and collect your mother? She has discharged herself." They made haste as one would, knowing pleasantries would be nonexistent on the ward.

The sister met them and said, "We thought she was a lovely lady when she came in but, my, she has changed."

Vera was a lovely lady, but Edward and Sylvia giggled knowing there had been a clash of personalities, and no one bossed Vera. A very worried Sylvia asked what food and drinks Vera was allowed, and was told nothing with any fat in it, although she did seem tolerant to milk—that was a huge relief.

Vera could have her cup of tea. That was half the battle as she loved the "cup that cheers" as she always called it. Whenever she went out—be it to friends or the cattle market, farm or furniture sales or services—she always loved a cuppa as soon as she got home. The sister informed them that Vera could have chicken, bread, and fruit, then to gradually try other nonfat foods.

There were problems to start with as Vera did not love vegetables, although she always grew a garden full of them; but eventually a diet was established, and Vera soon knew if she went off it as she had great discomfort and pain. Mr. Bell who had the Health Food Stores in Carlisle, was a great help and put Vera on Potters Gall Bladder Tablets; these were great as Vera had to be careful with fat in her diet for the rest of her life, and for years after if Vera ate something that gave her discomfort she would just go for her Gall Bladder Tablets. Then the government in all their wisdom banned one of the ingredients, "Kava Kava", declaring it unsafe. Well known people, even actresses, wrote articles in the papers and said how it had helped them, but The Gall Bladder Tablets had to go off the market.

Vera attended the Gospel Hall Hawick but from Newlands. This was a very long narrow winding road, not very nice in winter; it troubled Vera that attending a place of worship some distance from her home, her neighbours would not know of her faith and it would not have any influence on them. On a Sunday evening, she would attend the wee gathering at Roadhead, which was out in the country through the forestry towards Bewcastle. The congregation were mostly farmers at that time, meeting in an old schoolroom. Lay preachers who were sincere and faithful to what the scriptures taught came to take the services.

Once a year there was the special Roadhead Convention held in the Village Hall. A renowned speaker would come and there would be a soloist and a tea. When Vera was seventy five, she was sat in the congregation listening to the speaker when her daughter heard her make a strange noise. Looking at Vera, she saw her head was back over the seat, her hands clenched tightly across her chest, her fingers interlocked, her complexion was nearly black. Sylvia knew one of the local doctors was there, so she crept forward to Dr. Bethune and whispered to him about her mum. He went to Vera, cleared everyone off the seat, and laid Vera down. After a few minutes she opened her eyes and asked, "What's happened?"

The doctor whispered to keep quiet as the preacher was still speaking. As soon as he was able, he sat Vera up. He said she must go straight to the surgery in Newcastleton, as he was sure she had a minor stroke. This was to be the first of a few minor strokes in her lifetime. On Monday the family contacted Mr. Bell from the Carlisle Health Food Store again, who said she must go on Vitamin E, as it would help if there were any clots already there and help to prevent others forming, also help to keep her blood pressure down; these, but most of all her beloved Lord and Saviour, kept her healthy for many years. She had a few minor accidents but, on the whole, enjoyed good health.

Two things had happened that afternoon that upset Vera greatly. Though she was not often or easily disturbed, Vera was always busy and clean with food. When helping to prepare the food for the tea she saw another lady making sandwiches who kept licking her fingers, causing Vera great distress. Vera as already said had a beautiful singing voice. The soloist that afternoon could not reach the top notes easily and was harshly screeching them. Sylvia felt her mother shudder. These two things upset Vera very much.

The fires were all open at Newlands, apart from the Rayburn in the kitchen, so mostly wood was burnt. Edward placed eight parallel stakes in the ground about a foot apart; he placed branches and wood to be sawn for the fires between them; once he was sawing them with the chain saw, the branches he was sawing kept springing up, so he asked Vera to stand on them. Sylvia was hand washing clothes in the house when she heard Edward shouting for her. Dashing out of the house she saw her mother on the ground and a blood fountain going from her leg up to the Heavens. The saw blade had slid up her wellington and nearly severed her leg. Sylvia raced to the washing line and grabbed Vera's winceyette night dress, took the wellington off, and bound the nightie as tight as she could round Vera's leg. With the nightie being wet it was easy to get tight. Then she phoned the doctor's surgery. Mrs. Bethune said her husband was out, but she would contact him and told them to get Vera down to the surgery for when he arrived. Mrs. Bethune had great difficulty and was given to great mirth as she tried to cut through the nightie with a pair of scissors.

"Whatever is it?" she queried, though it had stopped the profuse bleeding. Vera was taken to hospital by ambulance to get the wound stitched and attended to; apart from a permanent scar, she recovered very well.

The land at Newlands just had wire fences, but at Hartoft, Vera was renowned for the way she kept the dry stone walls built up and in good condition. No National Parks or grants for building them then. It was just hard graft and Vera mended them all herself, indeed when she left Head House it was noted that not a wall was broken down. One farmer viewing said he had never seen walls in such good condition. Imagine Vera at Newlands many years with no walls and nearly eighty years old when part of a wall came down in a neighbour's field. It was down next to the road and the field had sheep in it. Noticing that neither the shepherd nor other farm hands did anything about it and fearing the sheep would get out, Vera went across and built it up. She was so pleased she could still do it although; she never received a word of thanks.

The district nurse called and said to Sylvia, who was working just inside the gate, "Can I speak to Mrs. Vera Stonehouse, please? I'm from the doctors and we have to check up on patients regularly when they reach the age of eighty."

"Well just wait here. She will be coming round the corner in a minute."

Soon Vera came hurrying with her jockey cap pushed back and carrying two large buckets of water.

"She can't be eighty years old! She looks younger than me," the nurse declared, and she did look a lot younger.

Newlands House had a large cottage in the grounds. Vera let this out to visitors on a holiday basis. When it was first furnished and ready for letting, Vera invited some farming friends, who were also in the holiday trade, to come for a holiday in the cottage—free of charge so long as they informed Vera if everything was there that was needed for a week or a fortnight's holiday. The night before they were leaving the wife whispered, "Could I have a quiet word with you? You asked me to let you know if there was anything essential you had forgot to put in the cottage."

"Yes."

"Well, there is not a fish slice."

Ever after a fish slice—be it in a shop or at a farm or house sale—became an article of great mirth for an eighty year old fantastic cook who had never used a fish slice in her life. Everything was tuned over or served with a large knife or spoon.

Chapter 19

THE FAMILY MOVE

IN 1982, VERA'S TWO BROTHERS AND SISTERS—who never married—lived and farmed at Lowdales Farm, Hackness, Nr Scarborough, came to retire in the Scottish Borders. They had been unable to farm for many years and had let the land off as summer grazing and a neighbour grew corn on the arable land. They had continued to live in the farmhouse with no running hot water, no electricity and no bathroom or WC and stone flag floors.

Vera had tried hard to persuade them for some time to move without success. They finally said if Vera could find them a nice house were they all had a bedroom each, which would be the first time for the sisters always slept in one room and the brothers in another, they also wanted about three acres of land to be able to keep their own cow, a Brethren Assembly where they had worshipped since children must be within three miles, and the property must be near the sea. Vera heard of the Old Manse at Kirkpatrick Fleming which met all their requirements. The Solway at Powfoot was near the sea, plus electricity, bathroom, and WC.

Edward went to fetch them to view the property since Vera's brother that drove was over eighty years old and had never driven long distances. Thinking how they had enjoyed the picturesque Lowdales valley for over forty years, he brought them the scenic route through Middleton in Teasdale on the narrow winding roads believing it would be more like home for them, especially knowing they had not been on motorways and may be afraid of all the heavy traffic. They had to travel both ways in the day. Having two dogs at home, so after they had viewed the property, and not shown much interest Edward took them home rather quickly via the A74 and A66. Vera phoned next day to see what they thought about it. They said the property and the area were fine, but it was that horrid road to it of course. They said if they purchased the place, they would not have to travel on it. It was a much nicer road Edward brought them home on. They did purchase it and with being an old manse they had to rename it. They called it Rosemount after Vera's youngest sister.

Vera went over from Newlands to prepare the place for them as it had not been lived in for some time. It was a distance of about twenty-four miles, so she stayed at the property and although in her seventies, scrubbed the place out from top to bottom, and also made a large impression on the large garden which was overgrown. It bore no resemblance of a garden; rubbish and weeds were taller than her. Vera went to King's Salerooms at Carlisle each week on the bus, as she knew their furniture had been in a working farmhouse therefore had been subject to knocks, coal fires, and woodworm. She purchased carpets, curtains, and furniture for the whole property, which had six bedrooms and two dressing rooms and bathroom upstairs. Downstairs, there were two large front rooms, a library, large kitchen, large pantry, another storeroom, a roomy cloakroom, and toilet. The flagged cellar was dry and usable. When Vera could not get on in the garden, she was making them curtains.

Vera had it looking lovely and photos were taken of the rooms and sent to her family so they would know what to bring. Vera told them to bring only essentials. They did send a lot to Boulton and Coopers Auction Rooms at Seamer Market but mostly small things clocks, silver, and ornaments and books.

When the furniture finally arrived Vera could not believe her eyes when they started to unload the shabby kitchen dressers, coil spring beds, and worn through horsehair sofas.

After Vera's brothers and sisters had sold the farm, before leaving day, Edward took William up to Vera at Kirkpatrick Fleming. He was causing problems with the clearing out and packing up, not wanting to part with possessions, going through boxes they had packed. When he arrived, he had a badly infected ulcer on his leg. Vera sterilized plantain leaves and put poultices on him, changing them every day. Plantain leaves were sterilized by pouring a kettle of boiling water over them. They have been known to cure gangrene.

The whole family preferred herbal cures to doctors' medicine whenever possible. Their grandmother on their mother's side, being a nurse before the days of modern medicine and chemicals, used a lot of herbs and even made her own salve that cured blood poisoning in wounds. William's leg healed up beautifully just like a baby's skin. Vera was delighted and thought William would be. Imagine her horror when many weeks later, when the rest of the family were at Rosemount and Vera visited them. William came to open the door with his trouser leg rolled up to the knee and putrid matter running down his leg.

"What have you done?" Vera cried.

Following her gaze, he said, "Oh that! I made a hole in my leg. I thought all that badness from the old ulcer must be going into my system and it should be coming out. It will be alright now. I've put some oil on it."

Vera asked, "What sort of oil?"

"Oh, from a tin of fish."

Vera knew when he was in that frame of mind it was useless to try again; it never did heal and was with him to the end—probably causing his sudden unexpected death.

While at Rosemount preparing for her family coming, Vera saw piles of old rubble around the front of the house. She sorted it, cleaned the bricks of any old cement, and made them into planters. With stones she found she made a rockery. Asking her daughter to bring her some plants, she was delighted as she got more ground cleared and more stones and bricks cleaned, and more planters erected. Vera eventually got all the rubble removed and as her daughter brought her more and more plants was delighted and tended her little flowers with the love and care she always put in her own gardens. Every house apart from the last two she had to set on and make a garden from nothing. if there had been a garden at some time, they were a wilderness before Vera moved in. When she had to start felling trees and tackling rubbish taller than herself, but she loved her gardens, seldom buying plants usually buying seeds or begging cuttings off shrubs and plants she saw and liked. Vera had green fingers and could make anything grow.

At Rosemount she carefully watered her plants at night and was looking forward to her sisters seeing the garden she had made. One morning she went into the garden and all her rockery and garden was covered with piles of the rubbish and weeds from her rubbish heap. She went in heartbroken.

"Will, have you seen what someone has done to my little plants and the garden?"

"Oh," he said, "I did that. There was a cold wind last night. I thought it would kill them."

Poor Vera. She tried hard to wade through the rubbish to find her little baby plants, but many were flattened or lost in their cruel onslaught from William.

Vera always loved rides out in the car. It did not matter if it was to the local shops, to see a friend, or to a service or sightseeing. She did not get out a lot but was never so happy as she was when travelling. It amused friends when visiting them. Soon after she got sat down, she would start to look at her watch ready for her ride home. Near or far, so long as the vehicle was moving, Vera was happy. She worked hard very hard often harder than any man and doing men's work too; it was lovely that she enjoyed these rides out and could really relax.

She loved picnics but hated cafes or restaurants and only about twice could be persuaded to go into them. This all stemmed from being given a dirty fork in a café just after she was married. Also, to Vera it was a waste of money since she was a very good cook. Why pay anyone else? She was a good steward but for most of her life until retiring was very careful with finance; the only exception to this rule was her Lord's work and this she supported as much as possible.

Vera's love of car travel was probably the fact that she worked hard often beyond her strength. If the journey was near or far it did not matter so long as the car wheels were moving. At Christian services and conferences in gospel halls, chapel services or sacred concerts, Vera was really happy; it was one time when she was not looking at her watch anticipating the ride home.

A cousin of Vera's used to come and stay, usually in May and September. Vera thought a lot about Albert. He lived in Nottingham and was at one time chief fire officer until his retirement. Vera had a problem tracing Albert. She decided she must trace some of her relatives while still living at Hartoft. She had fifty-two first cousins. With her father's relatives living in Yorkshire, she knew some of them but had lost all contact with her mother's side of the family, who were mostly in Nottinghamshire. Vera persuaded Edward to go to see if she could find some of them. The family set off early one morning after the farm and animals had been attended to. With no addresses, on arriving at Nottingham Vera went into a telephone box and phoned the fire station and asked to speak to her cousin, Albert Thornhill. The receptionist told her he had retired and was ex-directory.

Vera pleaded with the lady and told her she had travelled from Yorkshire to try and trace her relatives. So she said as he was retired there was no harm in her having his number. Finding the street and a beautiful house, Vera knocked on the door. Albert answered it.

They knew each other and were delighted.

"Come in and bring the family." Albert showed them into the lounge and immediately gave them a cup of tea. Many years later after asking Albert how he had made the tea so quickly he laughed and said his wife, Marjorie, had just gone visiting friends, so he had put the cricket on the TV and made a pot of tea when Vera knocked at the door hence the cuppa so readily available.

When Vera lived at Malton Cote, Ebberston, Albert—then a boy whose father died young in his thirties—came to stay on the farm. He cried the first half of the week because he wanted to go home and the second half because he wanted to stay. That was the first of many holidays on the farm. As a fourteen-year-old he cycled from Nottingham to Malton Cote for a holiday, then back home. The roads were not so busy then, but it was still a long way for a fourteen-year-old and on his own too.

Sadly, Albert developed dementia and not knowing such a thing existed, Vera could not understand his behaviour pattern in later life. On a holiday at Newlands one May, Edward, who with the family, put work aside for a few days to take them around to see local beauty spots and places of interest, told them when they came as usual in September he would like to take them to see Ullapool and Applecross. He had heard it was a delightful area. Vera was dumbfounded when as they were leaving to go home on the Saturday, Albert said "We will not be coming to see you in September. We are going to Ullapool."

It was not long after that Suzanne, Albert and Marjorie's daughter, phoned to say her parents would not be coming again to stay. Albert's driving licence had been taken away as he had dementia. This was a great sadness and heartache for Vera; one she felt deeply. It was not long before he and dear Marjorie were taken into care. Marjorie had a brain tumor which had, in turn, affected her seriously.

Edward did take Vera to Ullapool and the West Coast of Scotland right round the North Coast of Scotland with all its natural beauty. Its lovely little bays and inlets and hardly a soul to be seen, back down the East Coast, and home to Newlands all in one day.

Whilst driving up the steep incline at Applecross, Edward was a little uneasy about the steep sheer drop at the side of the road. All the time worried how Vera was feeling as the drop was at her side of the car.

All of a sudden, she exclaimed, "Oh look down there! There is an eagle!"

Edward said afterwards an eagle was the last thing on his mind. But Vera had not a care in the world. This was something she took all through her life. She had such a great love for her Lord and Saviour and such a trust in His keeping power that she was seldom afraid. It was a blessing to her family to be brought up in such an atmosphere.

Many a time Vera would say, "Just pray for me. I have to do this or that. Just pray for me. I have this awful pain. Just pray for me. I have to go in this field where the bull is. Just pray for me. I have to see the bank manager." Whatever the situation, it needed extra prayer; what a delightful way for her children to be brought up, knowing they could do nothing on their own they are completely reliant on their Heavenly Father and knowing by their mother's experience that His help is always there.

"And call upon me in the day of trouble: I will deliver thee, and thou shalt glorify me." Psalm 50:15.

Chapter 20

THURSO

THIS JOURNEY GAVE VERA a love for Scotland. Although already living in the Borders, she had not seen a lot of this magnificent country. Now being at Newlands for nearly fourteen years, Edward had been careful with his diet and his health had improved; he wanted to go farming again. Vera looked at several farm advertisements and selected one she would like to see and was given permission to view. Vera and Edward set off. Sylvia had no desire to go farming again. The local abattoirs were closing, and many animals were being shipped abroad and slaughtered inhumanely. The drivers of the cattle wagons stopped for scheduled breaks. The poor animals that had never been off the farm were fastened in the back of the lorry with hostile animals from other farms that they had never seen. At local abattoirs one knew the animals would be put down very soon and very quickly and humanely.

Vera was well on her way to view the farm when Sylvia received a phone call from the estate agents to say the farm had been withdrawn from sale. There was no way of contacting Vera. However, she did see another farm that was for sale which she and Edward liked and eventually purchased. Sylvia purchased a bungalow at Perth.

In July 1985, Vera's youngest sister Rosie passed away at aged 69. Her husband Eddie in August after a short illness—aged 79, his sister Grace—aged 69, and Vera's brother, William—aged 82—in that October. That meant there were just Vera's eldest brother and sister left in the Scottish Borders.

Vera purchased a lorry to move from Newlands to the farm at Thurso. There were twenty-seven loads, as some of the farm machinery had been retained at Newlands and some of the stock. Despite being over eighty years old, Vera helped load the lorry each time and unload them. Some of the contents were vehicle engines. She travelled with Edward for eighteen of the loads—a distance of over three hundred miles each way. Jean Scott, a neighbouring shepherd's wife, said she had always dreaded getting old but stopped worrying when Vera accomplished what she did at her age. Very sadly neither Jean or her husband saw old age.

The first hay time at Achverga, Edward came into the house and said he would have to purchase a big baler (they were just coming into fashion) next year as it was hard work leading hay on his own. He had to put so many bales up the elevator, then go up the ladder, and stack them.

"Well," said Vera, "maybe I could still put a few bales on the elevator for you."

Until leaving Hartoft, she put every bale on the elevator, but that was fourteen years since. She went out and, unknown to her, Edward kept a check. That year she put over a thousand bales on the elevator and she was over eighty years of age.

There was a large garden at Thurso and Vera dug it from wall to wall. She carried all the buckets of rubbish off, not digging it in like many do. Edward sowed the seed and they had some wonderful crops. There was also a flower garden which she dug, weeded, and kept very nice, as well as putting the wallpaper on in the house and preparing the meals.

Achverga was next to a quarry and there were some large heaps of shale (quarry waste). Vera carried buckets of it, from the field to the farm road to mend the potholes as they developed, thereby keeping the road in good condition.

In 1994, Vera's eldest surviving brother had a fall and was taken into Dumfries infirmary; he was 93 years old and at that time had been living with his sister, Lilian, at Rosemount, Kirkpatrick Fleming. Lilian, in a panic, phoned Vera. She had no way of going to see her brother. She had driven a car when younger but not for many years, although she still retained her driving license.

Sylvia went to stay with Lilian and took her every day to the hospital where unfortunately Everard was heavily drugged. There was no way a conversation could be held. Sadly, he passed away, after a month.

Lilian was alone now at Rosemount. Being a former manse, it was large roomy and draughty and lonely. Sylvia took her to view properties of manageable proportions—all to no avail as she had no intention of moving. Vera was worried about Lilian. She was vulnerable in this lonely house; she was no longer driving and was not on a bus route or near a shop. She had wonderful neighbours in John and Kath Richardson. John cut the lawns and Kath brought the shopping and coping with many helpful chores as she saw them needing doing. Christine Halliday and her sister Jackie, who grazed Lilian's paddocks, called in to see her when they could.

Sylvia had to go back to her own home from time to time. When at Lilian's, she took her to see properties although no way was Lilian moving. Then a property came on the market in Lockerbie, opposite the Brethren assembly where Lilian worshipped. They went to view it; there was a corner shop across the road selling bread and milk and essentials. It had a lovely large garden, garage, two coal houses, and a large shed. It had a granny flat and disused shop attached. She could have relatives take it in turn to come to the flat to help her, but no way was she moving.

Lilian was glued to her manse. Vera phoned at night to see how viewing had gone. When Sylvia told her the property was perfect for Lilian, Vera told her to put an offer in, for her.

"Would you like to move?" exclaimed a surprised Sylvia.

"I'd move tomorrow. Edward's been working on a neighbour's tractor for days and I hardly see him. He is always away doing something for someone. I have no near neighbours and I am sick of being on my own."

Sylvia put an offer in and gave the figure to the Lord to see if it was His will they move to Lockerbie. She had an idea of making the disused shop into a Christian bookshop. After a fortnight, the solicitor phoned to ask if they would go another six thousand pounds. They said no. They were Christians and had given the Lord that figure, saying if it came for that price, they would know it was His will they moved. Another fortnight elapsed and the solicitor phoned would they go another four thousand. They said no and they had already explained why. Two more weeks passed another phone call with the solicitor saying would they give another two thousand. He thought the vendors were being realistic.

Back came the reply, "Sorry, we dare not. If it does not come for our price, the Lord does not want us in Lockerbie."

Then the important call came "your offer has been accepted."

Chapter 21

BACK INTO CIVILISATION

VERA WAS NOW WELL INTO HER EIGHTIES, yet she packed all her own possessions for removal. She loved arranging her new home. The two houses had a covered passage between the two back doors which made the two houses like one. They could go down the short passage without having to put a coat on. Vera had great delight helping to start the Christian Book Shop and once the disused grocer's shop was altered and decorated, she was in her element. With being born in Driffield, she was used to town life; but had been in the country, sometimes miles from anywhere, for sixty years and not being able to drive, she had been dependent on others for transport all that time. Vera was a very able cyclist when she was younger, but this was not always convenient.

Vera walked to the shops every day; sometimes twice and was thrilled when she found a bargain. Once their own shop opened, she kept Sylvia supplied with cups of tea and lovely little snacks.

The shop soon had regular customers coming from Glasgow, Motherwell, Edinburgh, Devon, and Chester, as well as local customers. It specialised in the Authorised Version of the Bible; there was two racks of AV Bibles with different plans of study, different colours, different fastenings, and different bindings. Books, literature, greetings and Christmas cards all had AV texts. There was a large music selection with many out of print hymn books acquired from all over the world. Both the AV Bible and the good old Gospel Hymn Books were close to Vera's heart. It was not the intention for the shop to be a commercial proposition but that it would promote the Authorised Version and had gospel literature readily available.

Just inside the door was a large "free box", containing booklets, magazines, tracts, and Bibles. It was discovered that many people did not want something for nothing so a ten pence box was added, containing similar books; but people could leave ten pence if they chose to do so. While at the bookshop that there was an arson attack on the local school almost razing it to the ground. The Book Shop contacted their suppliers, and they willingly provided a large amount of Christian children's books to set up the library again; the school was delighted.

Nearly every customer was invited into Vera's front room for tea; she was quick to put the kettle on. Sylvia had strict instructions if anyone had travelled any distance and Vera was not in the shop to give her a ring on the phone. She loved entertaining all her life it was never any trouble to feed people.

"Distributing to the necessity of saints; given to hospitality." Romans 12:13.

Vera came back from the shops on one occasion, her face was badly bruised. She had fallen. Unfortunately, it was up an alley that was a short cut, and no one was about. She had to pick herself up and get home the best way she could; her Lord cared for her and she did not break any bones or even strain any limbs, but she did lose a bit of her confidence.

When Vera was eighty-eight, Sylvia married. She accepted this very well, despite always being rather a possessive mother. Davie, Sylvia's husband, booked a cottage in the Lake District with an extra bedroom and that took a dog when they got married. As Sylvia had hardly ever been separated from her mum, Vera never lived on her own, when told she could go with them, Vera said, "I have never slept in anyone else's bed and I am not going to start now."

After two years, Vera had a bad chest infection that turned to pneumonia. The doctor said she was too ill to be moved. She could not eat and drank very little. She could not get up from her bed. About two days later, she asked for some fresh air, so Sylvia helped her to the window. When Vera was safely back in bed, Sylvia fled downstairs and dropped on her knees and pleaded with the Lord to save Vera's life; she was so ill and weak.

Later that afternoon Vera requested she go downstairs for some proper fresh air. The stairs were very narrow and steep, so Sylvia went first and held on to the bannisters as tightly as she could, in case Vera slipped and fell; they had gone down a few steps when Vera shouted, "Get a move on, lass, don't take all day!"

Truly an answer to prayer.

". . .them that honour me I will honour. . ." 1 Samuel 2:30.

The family realised they would never be able to leave Vera anymore; although making a remarkable recovery, she never seemed as strong as in former times.

Vera had never had any holidays—only day trips to the Lake District or York and Hull. Davie had three holidays a year and was in the Male Voice Praise Movement attending festivals in various parts of the country, so a compromise had to be found. After a discussion Vera and Sylvia bought a bungalow with sea views in Scarborough from their friends, Edith and Pauline Uttley. Vera was quite willing to go on these holidays as she had her own bed. In fact, she so enjoyed her times in Scarborough, she went with Davie and Sylvia to Wales for the All Britain Male Voice Praise Festival; this was a breakthrough. Vera realised now she could not manage on her own and was quite willing to go on holidays—even sleeping in beds that were not her own. For several years she went to the Inverness MVP Festival with them sleeping in their rented chalet. To say, Vera never had a real holiday until she was nearly ninety, she really enjoyed them. Her last one being in Aberdeenshire two months before she went to be with her Lord. Vera was at the Aberdeen Male Voice

Praise Festival and they announced that they did not think they had ever had anyone a hundred years old in the congregation, certainly not one that had travelled so far to be there, for which she was given a round of applause.

On Vera's ninetieth birthday, her house in Lockerbie was filled with flowers and cards; although her actual birthday party was at Scarborough. There was a summer house in the garden. Davie and Sylvia got up early and decorated it, enlarging photos of Vera at various stages of her life, and fastening them to the walls along with the decorations. Crockery and cutlery and table linen were carefully carried in, the meal almost ready then her friends started to arrive John and Anne Keith whom she loved dearly—they were connected by marriage to Eddie's side of the family; Ken and Marion Watson from Ulrome, she had known the family nearly all of her life; Kens father Frank, his brothers, Tom and Jack, and sister Annie were all Methodists; they and Vera's family had some enjoyable musical evenings singing round the piano when they were young.

Once all had arrived in the house Davie said, "Let's go into the garden." Once in the garden, "This is the summer house. We'll have a look inside."

"Oh," Vera said. "I've never seen inside the summerhouse." And promptly went inside, saw the chairs, and sat down at the table so natural as if she had always done it.

Another friend of Vera's, although only four years younger than Vera, came from Pickering on the bus; afterwards Doris wanted to go up to the hospital to see her sister, so Davie took her up. He had put the car radio on and when he arrived back home, he said, "Put the TV on. Something dreadful has happened."

It was then heard that the dreadful incident of the aeroplanes being flown into the twin towers in America was revealed; always when mentioned, it is a reminder of the day Vera was ninety.

Chapter 22

THE LORD'S TO THE END

IT WAS IN 2003 THAT VERA MOVED with Davie and Sylvia to live in Scarborough; there were several deciding factors. Vera had very tall steep stairs in her house at Lockerbie and although no problem to go up them, the family were afraid she would trip, and fall down them. Also, Davie had a sinus and catarrh problem; when in Lockerbie he was choked up, but within two days of coming to Scarborough he was nearly clear.

Vera, although probably happiest living in Lockerbie, had some happy times in Scarborough. Davie was leader of York Male Voice. The choir practiced every fortnight on a Monday night. Vera loved these practices and the choirmen made so much of her. She loved hearing them sing. Vera went yearly to the Male Voice Praise Festivals in Bolton, Carlisle; she went to Banbury, Sutton Coldfield, and Derby, when they were held; she enjoyed some lovely singing, fellowship, teas, and suppers with the choirmen and their wives.

On moving to Scarborough, it was a great disappointment to Vera that her beloved Sacred Songs[1] and Solos Hymn Book had disappeared from the services, also the Redemption Songs. The NIV had replaced her faithful Authorised Version of the Bible; they said it was easier to understand, yet she understood her Authorised Version perfectly well as a child with a normal

---

1   *Sacred Songs and Solos, Twelve Hundred Hymns Compiled Under the Direction of Ira D Sankey,* Published by Marshall Morgan and Scott; and *Redemption Songs a Choice Collection of 1000 Hymns and Choruses for Evangelistic Meetings, Solo Singers, Choirs, and the Home,* Published by Pickering and Inglis Ltd.

education. The Believers Hymn Book had disappeared, taking away Vera's beloved old hymns and their deep meaning.

Vera had no near shops to walk to as in Lockerbie, although she was near her dear friend, Doris. She was also able to visit Hector and Brenda once more and sing the good old hymns in their home. Vera always gave her Heavenly Father His rightful place addressing Him as Thee and Thou and not trying to bring Him down to human level; this meant everything to Vera, who could never understand mere mortal man made from the dust of the earth addressing the one Almighty God and Creator of everything as "you".

One thing above all others that Vera taught her family by example, all big jobs had to be broken down into small ones. If there had been a lot of rain and there was a lot to do in the garden. She would dig or weed a small square, then do another one somewhere else, and bit by bit join the squares up until the job was finished. The family, as they grew older, found many tasks too difficult for them, then would think "what would Mam do?" Oh, yes, a little bit at a time; but persevere with the little bit at a time until the job was finished.

Vera never had much time for doctors and their drugs; her remedies came from the hedge bottoms. She had great faith in herbs, although there were a few remedies that Vera's medicine chest was never without: a jar of Vaseline, bottle of TCP, aspirins, olive oil, and peppermint oil. Any disinfecting was done with Jeyes Fluid.

When Vera was living in Driffield, she had a bad headache that would not go away; she eventually went to the chemist and he recommended a bottle of Mackenzie's Smelling Salts. It worked wonders for her, and she was never again without a bottle in her handbag. Plus, a packet of Victory V cough lozenges.

Vera began to experience difficulties walking to the shops at Lockerbie, though she never got to be unable to do it; she just had to keep stopping for a rest. The move to Scarborough was a good one in that respect.

Once again, although over ninety years of age, Vera did all her own packing. On the last night at Lockerbie, the furniture was packed into the lorries and sent off for delivery next day. Davie took some loads down in the car; they were leaving the next day with the last car full and Davie away with it.

Vera and Sylvia had got all cleaned up and with Trudy, their little dog, settled down for the night on two sun loungers in Vera's front room as the beds had gone. Sun loungers apparently are okay for a doze in the garden but not all night. After much tossing and turning, causing great hilarity—thankfully both could see the funny side of it—Sylvia noticed everything had gone quiet, yet she was still tossing and squirming about feeling springs and metal frames cutting in everywhere. They had a torch each as the bedside lights had gone. So putting on the torch, she saw Vera had taken the mattress off the frame and put it on the floor and was lying on it, fast asleep. Vera still had all the brains at ninety-three. Sylvia did likewise and on waking in the morning, Trudy was lying happily between them.

Being a town girl moving to isolated farms in her twenties, she was happy at Scarborough. She was happy to attend sacred concerts in chapels and had many friends there. Vera was not exclusive; she had time for everyone.

Sitting in the car waiting for the open air meeting to start one Sunday evening, women in various forms of "undress", people staggering all over the place swigging bottles of alcohol, cursing and bitterness pouring from their mouths, Vera remarked to her companions, "Won't hell be a dreadful place?"

Someone said, "Well most Christians are no beauties."

"Ahh," she replied, "but we shall be changed." She knew her Bible well.

At Scarborough, Vera loved to sit in the window and watch the ships on the sea, neighbours in their gardens, and going in and out in their cars. There was no twitching of curtains. They knew she was there and gave her a wave. The postmen changed frequently, but most gave Vera a wave and a friendly smile as they delivered the mail.

Vera's later years were spent doing puzzles. First crosswords and later word searches; she loved her Rubik's cube which she did right up to the last month of her life. She read a lot in her younger days.

Vera's days always began and ended on her knees in prayer with her beloved Lord. Many the arrow prayer that ascended during the days and nights, any problem or difficulty it was always: "I've taken it to the Lord". Anyone else with a problem: "Pray about it". On joyous occasions when much blessing had been received or as soon as prayers were answered: "Isn't the Lord good?"

Her Heavenly Father meant everything to Vera; her Lord and Saviour very precious, she did not buttonhole people with her faith, but my word she prayed for them, knowing they were not capable of dragging themselves out of sin, but her Lord was.

That Vera was led so much in her life by the Holy Spirit was never in any doubt; although like David in Scripture, self would rise, but not often and not for long. And Vera was very sorry and repentant afterwards. Vera's Lord and Saviour died; He gave His life for her sins. She never forgot to thank Him, but never thought she did enough for Him or praised Him enough. Oh, how she used to love to sing for Him, with that beautiful voice He gave her.

While at Lockerbie when Sylvia was busy in the shop, Vera would phone friends, and as friends passed away, she would phone her friends children. She had many happy times looking up phone numbers of friends and ringing them—friends she had not seen for many years and giving them a call. Then her hearing began to fail, she was given a hearing aid, but did not cope with it very well; by the time she came to Scarborough, she could not hear on the phone anymore.

Chapter 23

NEARER MY GOD TO THEE

AT NINETY-SIX YEARS OF AGE, Vera had a successful cataract operation. It was a difficult operation for the surgeon; so difficult he refused to do her other eye saying she would not go blind as she would always have sight in one eye. It made a great difference to Vera.

In the October of her ninety-seventh year, Vera got up one morning with dreadful pain in her head. She could not bear the light, either from the window, electric light, or fire. Aspirins, darkening the room, bathing her feet in warm water—nothing worked nor made her feel any better. The doctor said it was temporal arteritis and there was not a cure. He could put her on steroids, but she would be on them for five years at least, if they worked. He said he would try them for three days, by that time we would know if they were going to work and she could still come off them if they didn't. After three days, there was no difference, so the doctor took her off them.

From October to February, Vera was in agony with her head. Davie heard that Naturopath Jan De Vries was on the radio on a Friday morning; he phoned in and explained that Vera was ninety-seven and had terrible pains in her head since October.

"Oh," he replied "That will be Temporal Arteritis. Go to your local Health Food Store and buy Vogels Knotgrass and give her fifteen drops night and morning. The knotgrass was purchased and administered that night and on the Tuesday morning Vera said, "Come here. Look at all these birds on this

219

telephone line." Not only was she taking notice, she was looking out of the window in broad daylight without any pain.

Vera enjoyed good health for a while and was able to go to the choir practices and festivals, sacred concerts at chapels, and touring, even holidays.

Arriving home from one choir practice, Vera was drinking a cup of tea; she always loved another cup of tea when she got home, even if she had just had supper with friends. Davie called to Sylvia in the kitchen to say something had gone wrong with Vera and she had knocked her tea over. Vera did not respond when spoken to or touched, although still sitting.

Davie whispered, "I'm going to phone the doctor. Mum's had a stroke." He was put through to a nurse who said she would send an ambulance.

"Oh no, my wife has promised her mum she will never send her to hospital. Her mother, father, brother, and sister all died of pneumonia contracted in the hospital so she made Sylvia promise she would never send her. I require a doctor at the house" After a long argument Davie received the promise of a house visit from a doctor. The nurse had told him that Vera would be better in bed. Vera could not walk or talk so Davie fetched the wheelchair which he used for Vera if she had to walk any distance.

Once in bed, Sylvia, tears raining down her face, knelt by Vera's bedside and pleaded with the Lord to heal her mum.

She got up and was going out of the door when a voice said loud and clear, "What happened?"

Turning around she saw Vera looking normal, smiling as usual.

"You've had a slight turn, Mum, but you're ok now."

"Can I have a cup of tea?"

"Sure, Davies just made one."

This scene greeted the out of hours doctor when he walked in. Vera sat up in bed with a cup of tea and a big smile. He was quite indignant, "She's never had a stroke!"

"Well she could not speak, only to slur her words, could not stand, her mouth was twisted, and she had no use in one hand. That must be a stroke."

No one had the heart to tell him Vera's other hand was very strong; she always carried a large handbag and was never far from it. For most of her life, if it was out of sight it was only for a few seconds.

"Where's my handbag?"

This was to be expected as when she was farming everything was in it; cheque books were large then, so were farmhouse keys. Vera must have felt something when the stroke was coming on, as her good hand was tightly clenched round the handbag handle no one could prize it out when putting her into bed.

The doctor took a large A4 sheet of paper out and began to write and write. "Send for Vera's own doctor in the morning and give him this."

When he had departed the note was read, "Refused Ambulance, Refused Hospital treatment, etc. etc."

Sylvia said, "Pray she lives. I will have to hang with a doctor's note like this."

Vera's own Dr. Hughes arrived in the morning and burst out laughing when he read the note. The family told him if Vera had gone to hospital she would probably be placed in a side ward, and with it being the early hours—it was twelve thirty in the morning—and a shortage of staff she could have been left alone, come around, been frightened, and had a massive stroke.

Vera enjoyed many more holidays and outings and was approaching her hundredth birthday. A lady from the pension office called in July. She needed details both for the card from the Queen and to see if Vera was eligible for anymore pension.

"When did Vera last see a doctor?"

Everyone looked at each other, not having a clue. That afternoon a phone call came from the doctors' surgery, asking for Vera to go in for a medical review. Sylvia asked the doctor when Vera had last seen a doctor. He looked at his computer and said October, so at over ninety-nine years of age. Vera had not needed to see a doctor for nine months.

It was decided to have the birthday celebrations over a fortnight so as not to confuse Vera with a sea of faces. Vera's closest friend, Doris Nesfield, who used to farm at High Langdale End, was brought over in the morning by her daughter, Jean, for the photographs. Doris herself was ninety-five years old. Also, cousin Basil and his wife, Mary, who farm at Staxton near Scarborough. Vera always thought a lot about Basil's mother. Methodist Minister Peter Cross, then of Scarborough and choir leader and dear friend John Woodmansey, brought a magnificent basket of flowers which lasted for weeks and was the centre piece of most of the photos. Relatives and friends came throughout the day.

Hundreds of cards were received as well as the special one from HRH, letters of Greetings and many Bouquets and Boxes of Chocolates.

For many years, Wrelton Methodist Chapel had an annual visit in September from the Staithes Fishermens Choir. Vera used to love to hear them when she farmed at Hartoft, only about six miles away. It was always around Vera's birthday. They gave a concert, singing many of the good old hymns and a lovely supper was provided. John Lumley and the dear folk at Wrelton included Vera for her ninety-eighth, ninety-ninth, and hundredth birthdays; the family took a birthday cake.

After preparing the food for the supper and for the choir practice to be held one night at the end of September, Sylvia took Vera's tea through to her in the living room; she noticed a large man's handkerchief wrapped round Vera's hand, which she was trying to hide up her sleeve.

"What's the matter with your hand, Mam?"

"Nothing."

"Come on, Mam, let me have a look."

"It's nothing."

On undoing the handkerchief, there was a large triangle of skin torn on the back of Vera's hand.

"What have you done, Mum?"

"I don't know."

Then Sylvia remembered taking a hot tray from the oven and nearly falling over dear Trudy, the beloved family pet. She let out a yell and poor Trudy fled from the kitchen. She must have raced through and jumped on Vera's knee, where she spent a lot of time, catching her hand in the process. Vera loved the choir practices and being desperate to go had realised if she needed medical attention she may not be able to go, it was almost five o'clock and the car left at six; so being Vera, she decided to grin and bear the pain and she had it hidden where no one would see it.

Sylvia phoned Davie, who had not arrived home, and said Vera must go to the doctor immediately. Davie phoned the surgery, explaining that they should be leaving for the choir practice which was forty-two miles away at York and he was the leader and had the key. They took Vera down, although it was surgery the nurse took Vera straight away and said she would try and get the skin to heal if possible. Vera had to go every day to have it dressed and was put on antibiotics; Vera got to hear her much loved practice and the large wound healed beautifully.

A short time later, Vera got chest infection which would not clear. The doctor put her on another course of antibiotics; it was not known if it was the antibiotics, or if Vera had suffered another slight stroke, but she never ate a proper meal again. Tempting snacks were cooked, but she would not taste them; and yet she still was delighted to go out in the car.

One of the first things she said on a morning, "Are we going anywhere today?"

When Sylvia put her to bed at night Vera would say, "What can I do for you honey? You are so good to me."

"Just eat, Mam."

"I am eating honey."

"Mam, you have not had a crumb today."

"Oh, well, I'll eat tomorrow."

The doctor said she would have to go to hospital, and they would put her on drip. Sylvia went with her, as she promised her mum, she would never send her to hospital; she felt it was not sending her mum to Hospital if she was with her, and sat at her bedside for three weeks, but Vera never fully recovered consciousness. Davie did a sterling work keeping the washing in hand and bringing meals to the hospital for Sylvia and looking after Trudy.

One night a lovely nurse, Morag, came to say goodbye to Vera. She was going off duty for several days. She brought another nurse, who would be on Vera's ward.

Sylvia said, "I wish you could have heard Mum sing. She has a beautiful voice and has sung all over in places of worship."

Just then Vera in her beautiful clear sweet voice started to sing her favourite solo. She sung it right through every verse and chorus.

> **Oh my Redeemer, What a Friend Thou art to me!**
> **Oh what a refuge I have found in Thee!**
> **When the way was dreary, and my heart was sore oppressed,**
> **Twas Thy voice that lulled me, to a calm sweet rest.**
>
> **Nearer, draw nearer,**
> **Till my soul be lost in Thee:**
> **Nearer, draw nearer,**
> **Blessed Lord to Thee.**
>
> **When in their beauty, stars unveil their silver light,**
> **Then o my Saviour, give me songs at night-**
> **Songs of yonder mansions, where the dear ones gone before,**
> **Sing Thy praise for ever, On that peaceful shore.**

Jesus my saviour, When the last deep shadows fall;

When in the silence, I shall hear thy call-

In thine arms reposing, let me breathe my life away,

And awake triumphant, In eternal day.

The next morning when the day nurse came on duty, the night nurse said, "You should have been here last night when I came on duty. Vera sang for me."

Where upon once again, Vera sang the words that meant so much to her. It was not just the words she knew; it was her Saviour.

Tell Mother I'll be there, in answer to her prayer;

This message blessed Saviour to her bear.

Tell mother I'll be there, Heavens joys with her to share,

Yes, tell my darling Mother, I'll be there.

I would like to say thank you to my brother for his commitment and help with the ancestry for this book. And I would also like to thank my husband for diligently helping me complete the manuscript.

—Sylvia

For more information about

Sylvia Lindsay
and
Have I Ever Told You?

please visit:

www.ambassador-international.com
@AmbassadorIntl
www.facebook.com/AmbassadorIntl

If you enjoyed this book, please consider leaving us a review on Amazon, Goodreads, or our website.

Printed in Poland
by Amazon Fulfillment
Poland Sp. z o.o., Wrocław

57144468R00130